Letters on Lit

Andrew Lang

Alpha Editions

This edition published in 2022

ISBN : 9789356783164

Design and Setting By
Alpha Editions
www.alphaedis.com
Email - info@alphaedis.com

Contents

PREFACE

These Letters were originally published in the *Independent* of New York. The idea of writing them occurred to the author after he had produced "Letters to Dead Authors." That kind of Epistle was open to the objection that nobody *would* write so frankly to a correspondent about his own work, and yet it seemed that the form of Letters might be attempted again. The *Lettres à Emilie sur la Mythologie* are a well-known model, but Emilie was not an imaginary correspondent. The persons addressed here, on the other hand, are all people of fancy—the name of Lady Violet Lebas is an invention of Mr. Thackeray's: gifted Hopkins is the minor poet in Dr. Oliver Wendell Holmes's "Guardian Angel." The author's object has been to discuss a few literary topics with more freedom and personal bias than might be permitted in a graver kind of essay. The Letter on Samuel Richardson is by a lady more frequently the author's critic than his collaborator.

INTRODUCTORY: OF MODERN ENGLISH POETRY

To Mr. Arthur Wincott, Topeka, Kansas.

Dear Wincott,—You write to me, from your "bright home in the setting sun," with the flattering information that you have read my poor "Letters to Dead Authors." You are kind enough to say that you wish I would write some "Letters to Living Authors;" but that, I fear, is out of the question,—for me.

A thoughtful critic in the *Spectator* has already remarked that the great men of the past would not care for my shadowy epistles—if they could read them. Possibly not; but, like Prior, "I may write till they can spell"—an exercise of which ghosts are probably as incapable as was Matt's little Mistress of Quality. But Living Authors are very different people, and it would be perilous, as well as impertinent, to direct one's comments on them literally, in the French phrase, "to their address." Yet there is no reason why a critic should not adopt the epistolary form.

Our old English essays, the papers in the *Tatler* and *Spectator*, were originally nothing but letters. The vehicle permits a touch of personal taste, perhaps of personal prejudice. So I shall write my "Letters on Literature," of the present and of the past, English, American, ancient, or modern, to *you*, in your distant Kansas, or to such other correspondents as are kind enough to read these notes.

Poetry has always the precedence in these discussions. Poor Poetry! She is an ancient maiden of good family, and is led out first at banquets, though many would prefer to sit next some livelier and younger Muse, the lady of fiction, or even the chattering *soubrette* of journalism. *Seniores priores*. Poetry, if no longer very popular, is a dame of the worthiest lineage, and can boast a long train of gallant admirers, dead and gone. She has been much in courts. The old Greek tyrants loved her; great Rhamses seated her at his right hand; every prince had his singers. Now we dwell in an age of democracy, and Poetry wins but a feigned respect, more out of courtesy, and for old friendship's sake, than for liking. Though so many write verse, as in Juvenal's time, I doubt if many read it. "None but minstrels list of sonneting." The purchasing public, for poetry, must now consist chiefly of poets, and *they* are usually poor.

Can anything speak more clearly of the decadence of the art than the birth of so many poetical "societies"? We have the Browning Society, the Shelley

Society, the Shakespeare Society, the Wordsworth Society—lately dead. They all demonstrate that people have not the courage to study verse in solitude, and for their proper pleasure; men and women need confederates in this adventure. There is safety in numbers, and, by dint of tea-parties, recitations, discussions, quarrels and the like, Dr. Furnivall and his friends keep blowing the faint embers on the altar of Apollo. They cannot raise a flame!

In England we are in the odd position of having several undeniable poets, and very little new poetry worthy of the name. The chief singers have outlived, if not their genius, at all events its flowering time. Hard it is to estimate poetry, so apt we are, by our very nature, to prefer "the newest songs," as Odysseus says men did even during the war of Troy. Or, following another ancient example, we say, like the rich niggards who neglected Theocritus, "Homer is enough for all."

Let us attempt to get rid of every bias, and, thinking as dispassionately as we can, we still seem to read the name of Tennyson in the golden book of English poetry. I cannot think that he will ever fall to a lower place, or be among those whom only curious students pore over, like Gower, Drayton, Donne, and the rest. Lovers of poetry will always read him as they will read Wordsworth, Keats, Milton, Coleridge, and Chaucer. Look his defects in the face, throw them into the balance, and how they disappear before his merits! He is the last and youngest of the mighty race, born, as it were, out of due time, late, and into a feebler generation.

Let it be admitted that the gold is not without alloy, that he has a touch of voluntary affectation, of obscurity, even an occasional perversity, a mannerism, a set of favourite epithets ("windy" and "happy"). There is a momentary echo of Donne, of Crashaw, nay, in his earliest pieces, even a touch of Leigh Hunt. You detect it in pieces like "Lilian" and "Eleanore," and the others of that kind and of that date.

Let it be admitted that "In Memoriam" has certain lapses in all that meed of melodious tears; that there are trivialities which might deserve (here is an example) "to line a box," or to curl some maiden's locks, that there are weaknesses of thought, that the poet now speaks of himself as a linnet, singing "because it must," now dares to approach questions insoluble, and again declines their solution. What is all this but the changeful mood of grief? The singing linnet, like the bird in the old English heathen apologue, dashes its light wings painfully against the walls of the chamber into which it has flown out of the blind night that shall again receive it.

I do not care to dwell on the imperfections in that immortal strain of sympathy and consolation, that enchanted book of consecrated regrets. It is an easier if not more grateful task to note a certain peevish egotism of tone in the heroes of "Locksley Hall," of "Maud," of "Lady Clara Vere de Vere." "You can't think how poor a figure you make when you tell that story, sir," said Dr. Johnson to some unlucky gentleman whose "figure" must certainly have been more respectable than that which is cut by these whining and peevish lovers of Maud and Cousin Amy.

Let it be admitted, too, that King Arthur, of the "Idylls," is like an Albert in blank verse, an Albert cursed with a Guinevere for a wife, and a Lancelot for friend. The "Idylls," with all their beauties, are full of a Victorian respectability, and love of talking with Vivien about what is not so respectable. One wishes, at times, that the "Morte d'Arthur" had remained a lonely and flawless fragment, as noble as Homer, as polished as Sophocles. But then we must have missed, with many other admirable things, the "Last Battle in the West."

People who come after us will be more impressed than we are by the Laureate's versatility. He has touched so many strings, from "Will Waterproof's Monologue," so far above Praed, to the agony of "Rizpah," the invincible energy of "Ulysses," the languor and the fairy music of the "Lotus Eaters," the grace as of a Greek epigram which inspires the lines to Catullus and to Virgil. He is with Milton for learning, with Keats for magic and vision, with Virgil for graceful recasting of ancient golden lines, and, even in the latest volume of his long life, "we may tell from the straw," as Homer says, "what the grain has been."

There are many who make it a kind of religion to regard Mr. Browning as the greatest of living English poets. For him, too, one is thankful as for a veritable great poet; but can we believe that impartial posterity will rate him with the Laureate, or that so large a proportion of his work will endure? The charm of an enigma now attracts students who feel proud of being able to understand what others find obscure. But this attraction must inevitably become a stumbling-block.

Why Mr. Browning is obscure is a long question; probably the answer is that he often could not help himself. His darkest poems may be made out by a person of average intelligence who will read them as hard as, for example, he would find it necessary to read the "Logic" of Hegel. There is a story of two clever girls who set out to peruse "Sordello," and corresponded with each other about their progress. "Somebody is dead in 'Sordello,'" one of them wrote to her friend. "I don't quite know *who* it is, but it must make things a little clearer in the long run." Alas! a copious use of the guillotine would scarcely clear the stage of "Sordello." It is hardly to be hoped that "Sordello," or "Red Cotton Night Cap Country," or "Fifine," will continue to be struggled with by posterity. But the mass of "Men and Women," that unexampled gallery of portraits of the inmost hearts and secret minds of priests, prigs, princes, girls, lovers, poets, painters, must survive immortally, while civilization and literature last, while men care to know what is in men.

No perversity of humour, no voluntary or involuntary harshness of style, can destroy the merit of these poems, which have nothing like them in the letters of the past, and must remain without successful imitators in the future. They will last all the better for a certain manliness of religious faith—something sturdy and assured—not moved by winds of doctrine, not paltering with doubts, which is certainly one of Mr. Browning's attractions in this fickle and shifting generation. He cannot be forgotten while, as he says—

> "A sunset touch,
> A chorus ending of Euripides,"

remind men that they are creatures of immortality, and move "a thousand hopes and fears."

If one were to write out of mere personal preference, and praise most that which best fits one's private moods, I suppose I should place Mr. Matthew Arnold at the head of contemporary English poets. Reason and reflection, discussion and critical judgment, tell one that he is not quite there.

Mr. Arnold had not the many melodies of the Laureate, nor his versatile mastery, nor his magic, nor his copiousness. He had not the microscopic glance of Mr. Browning, nor his rude grasp of facts, which tears the life out of them as the Aztec priest plucked the very heart from the victim. We know that, but yet Mr. Arnold's poetry has our love; his lines murmur in our memory through all the stress and accidents of life. "The Scholar Gipsy," "Obermann," "Switzerland," the melancholy majesty of the close of "Sohrab and Rustum," the tenderness of those elegiacs on two kindred graves beneath the Himalayas and by the Midland Sea; the surge and thunder of "Dover Beach," with its "melancholy, long-withdrawing roar;" these can only cease to whisper to us and console us in that latest hour when life herself ceases to "moan round with many voices."

My friends tell me that Mr. Arnold is too doubting, and too didactic, that he protests too much, and considers too curiously, that his best poems are, at most, "a chain of highly valuable thoughts." It may be so; but he carries us back to "wet, bird-haunted English lawns;" like him "we know what white and purple fritillaries the grassy harvest of the river yields," with him we try to practise resignation, and to give ourselves over to that spirit

> "Whose purpose is not missed,
> While life endures, while things subsist."

Mr. Arnold's poetry is to me, in brief, what Wordsworth's was to his generation. He has not that inspired greatness of Wordsworth, when nature does for him what his "*lutin*" did for Corneille, "takes the pen from his hand and writes for him." But he has none of the creeping prose which, to my poor mind, invades even "Tintern Abbey." He is, as Mr. Swinburne says, "the surest-footed" of our poets. He can give a natural and lovely life even to the wildest of ancient imaginings, as to "these bright and ancient snakes, that once were Cadmus and Harmonia."

Bacon speaks of the legends of the earlier and ruder world coming to us "breathed softly through the flutes of the Grecians." But even the Grecian flute, as in the lay of the strife of Apollo and Marsyas, comes more tunably in the echo of Mr. Arnold's song, that beautiful song in "Empedocles on Etna," which has the perfection of sculpture and the charm of the purest colour. It is full of the silver light of dawn among the hills, of the music of the loch's dark, slow waves among the reeds, of the scent of the heather, and the wet tresses of the birch.

Surely, then, we have had great poets living among us, but the fountains of their song are silent, or flow but rarely over a clogged and stony channel. And who is there to succeed the two who are gone, or who shall be our poet, if the Master be silent? That is a melancholy question, which I shall try to answer (with doubt and dread enough) in my next letter. {1}

OF MODERN ENGLISH POETRY

My dear Wincott,—I hear that a book has lately been published by an American lady, in which all the modern poets are represented. The singers have been induced to make their own selections, and put forward, as Mr. Browning says, their best foot, anapæst or trochee, or whatever it may be. My information goes further, and declares that there are but eighteen poets of England to sixty inspired Americans.

This Western collection of modern minstrelsy shows how very dangerous it is to write even on the English poetry of the day. Eighteen is long odds against a single critic, and Major Bellenden, in "Old Mortality," tells us that three to one are odds as long as ever any warrior met victoriously, and that warrior was old Corporal Raddlebanes.

I decline the task; I am not going to try to estimate either the eighteen of England or the sixty of the States. It is enough to speak about three living poets, in addition to those masters treated of in my last letter. Two of the three you will have guessed at—Mr. Swinburne and Mr. William Morris. The third, I dare say, you do not know even by name. I think he is not one of the English eighteen—Mr. Robert Bridges. His muse has followed the epicurean maxim, and chosen the shadowy path, *fallentis semita vitæ*, where the dew lies longest on the grass, and the red rowan berries droop in autumn above the yellow St. John's wort. But you will find her all the fresher for her country ways.

My knowledge of Mr. William Morris's poetry begins in years so far away that they seem like reminiscences of another existence. I remember sitting beneath Cardinal Beaton's ruined castle at St. Andrews, looking across the bay to the sunset, while some one repeated "Two Red Roses across the Moon." And I remember thinking that the poem was nonsense. With Mr. Morris's other early verses, "The Defence of Guinevere," this song of the moon and the roses was published in 1858. Probably the little book won no attention; it is not popular even now. Yet the lyrics remain in memories which forget all but a general impression of the vast "Earthly Paradise," that huge decorative poem, in which slim maidens and green-clad men, and waters wan, and flowering apple trees, and rich palaces are all mingled as on some long ancient tapestry, shaken a little by the wind of death. They are not living and breathing people, these persons of the fables; they are but shadows, beautiful and faint, and their poem is fit reading for sleepy summer afternoons. But the characters in the lyrics in "The Defence of Guinevere" are people of flesh and blood, under their chain armour and their velvet, and the trappings of their tabards.

There is no book in the world quite like this of Mr. Morris's old Oxford days when the spirit of the Middle Ages entered into him, with all its contradictions of faith and doubt, and its earnest desire to enjoy this life to the full in war and love, or to make certain of a future in which war is not, and all love is pure heavenly. If one were to choose favourites from "The Defence of Guinevere," they would be the ballads of "Shameful Death," and of "The Sailing of the Sword," and "The Wind," which has the wind's wail in its voice, and all the mad regret of "Porphyria's Lover" in its burden.

The use of "colour-words," in all these pieces, is very curious and happy. The red ruby, the brown falcon, the white maids, "the scarlet roofs of the good town," in "The Sailing of the Sword," make the poem a vivid picture. Then look at the mad, remorseful sea-rover, the slayer of his lady, in "The Wind":

> "For my chair is heavy and carved, and with sweeping green behind
> It is hung, and the dragons thereon grin out in the gusts of the wind;
> On its folds an orange lies with a deep gash cut in the rind;
> If I move my chair it will scream, and the orange will roll out far,
> And the faint yellow juice ooze out like blood from a wizard's jar,
> And the dogs will howl for those who went last month the war."

"The Blue Closet," which is said to have been written for some drawings of Mr. Rossetti, is also a masterpiece in this romantic manner. Our brief English age of romanticism, our 1830, was 1856-60, when Mr. Morris, Mr. Burne Jones, and Mr. Swinburne were undergraduates. Perhaps it wants a peculiar turn of taste to admire these strange things, though "The Haystack in the Floods," with its tragedy, must surely appeal to all who read poetry.

For the rest, as time goes on, I more and more feel as if Mr. Morris's long later poems, "The Earthly Paradise" especially, were less art than "art manufacture." This may be an ungrateful and erroneous sentiment. "The Earthly Paradise," and still more certainly "Jason," are full of such pleasure as only poetry can give. As some one said of a contemporary politician, they are "good, but copious." Even from narrative poetry Mr. Morris has long abstained. He, too, illustrates Mr. Matthew Arnold's parable of "The Progress of Poetry."

> "The Mount is mute, the channel dry."

Euripides has been called "the meteoric poet," and the same title seems very appropriate to Mr. Swinburne. Probably few readers had heard his name—I only knew it as that of the author of a strange mediæval tale in prose—when he published "Atalanta in Calydon" in 1865. I remember taking up the quarto in white cloth, at the Oxford Union, and being instantly led captive by the beauty and originality of the verse.

There was this novel "meteoric" character in the poem: the writer seemed to rejoice in snow and fire, and stars, and storm, "the blue cold fields and folds of air," in all the primitive forces which were alive before this earth was; the naked vast powers that circle the planets and farthest constellations. This quality, and his varied and sonorous verse, and his pessimism, put into the mouth of a Greek chorus, were the things that struck one most in Mr. Swinburne. He was, above all, "a mighty-mouthed inventer of harmonies," and one looked eagerly for his next poems. They came with disappointment and trouble.

The famous "Poems and Ballads" have become so well known that people can hardly understand the noise they made. I don't wonder at the scandal, even now. I don't see the fun of several of the pieces, except the mischievous fun of shocking your audience. However, "The Leper" and his company are chiefly boyish, in the least favourable sense of the word. They do not destroy the imperishable merit of the "Hymn to Proserpine" and the "Garden of Proserpine" and the "Triumph of Time" and "Itylus."

Many years have passed since 1866, and yet one's old opinion, that English poetry contains no verbal music more original, sonorous, and sweet than Mr. Swinburne wrote in these pieces when still very young, remains an opinion unshaken. Twenty years ago, then, he had enabled the world to take his measure; he had given proofs of a true poet; he was learned too in literature as few poets have been since Milton, and, like Milton, skilled to make verse in the languages of the ancient world and in modern tongues. His French songs and Greek elegiacs are of great excellence; probably no scholar who was not also a poet could match his Greek lines on Landor.

What, then, is lacking to make Mr. Swinburne a poet of a rank even higher than that which he occupies? Who can tell? There is no science that can master this chemistry of the brain. He is too copious. "Bothwell" is long enough for six plays, and "Tristram of Lyonesse" is prolix beyond even mediæval narrative. He is too pertinacious; children are the joy of the world and Victor Hugo is a great poet; but Mr. Swinburne almost makes us excuse Herod and Napoleon III. by his endless odes to Hugo, and rondels to small boys and girls. *Ne quid nimis*, that is the golden rule which he constantly spurns, being too luxuriant, too emphatic, and as fond of repeating himself as Professor Freeman. Such are the defects of so noble a genius; thus perverse Nature has decided that it shall be, Nature which makes no ruby without a flaw.

The name of Mr. Robert Bridges is probably strange to many lovers of poetry who would like nothing better than to make acquaintance with his verse. But his verse is not so easily found. This poet never writes in magazines; his books have not appealed to the public by any sort of advertisement, only two or three of them have come forth in the regular way. The first was "Poems, by Robert Bridges, Batchelor of Arts in the University of Oxford. *Parva seges satis est.* London: Pickering, 1873."

This volume was presently, I fancy, withdrawn, and the author has distributed some portions of it in succeeding pamphlets, or in books printed at Mr. Daniel's private press in Oxford. In these, as in all Mr. Bridges's poems, there is a certain austere and indifferent beauty of diction and a memory of the old English poets, Milton and the earlier lyrists. I remember being greatly pleased with the "Elegy on a Lady whom Grief for the Death of Her Betrothed Killed."

> "Let the priests go before, arrayed in white,
>   And let the dark-stoled minstrels follow slow
> Next they that bear her, honoured on this night,
>   And then the maidens in a double row,
>   Each singing soft and low,
> And each on high a torch upstaying:
> Unto her lover lead her forth with light,
> With music and with singing, and with praying."

This is a stately stanza.

In his first volume Mr. Bridges offered a few rondeaux and triolets, turning his back on all these things as soon as they became popular. In spite of their popularity I have the audacity to like them still, in their humble twittering way. Much more in his true vein were the lines, "Clear and Gentle Stream," and all the other verses in which, like a true Etonian, he celebrates the beautiful Thames:

> "There is a hill beside the silver Thames,
>   Shady with birch and beech and odorous pine,
> And brilliant under foot with thousand gems
>   Steeply the thickets to his floods decline.
>   Straight trees in every place
>   Their thick tops interlace,
>   And pendent branches trail their foliage fine
>   Upon his watery face.

* * * * *

A reedy island guards the sacred bower
  And hides it from the meadow, where in peace
The lazy cows wrench many a scented flower,
  Robbing the golden market of the bees.
    And laden branches float
    By banks of myosote;
  And scented flag and golden fleur-de-lys
    Delay the loitering boat."

I cannot say how often I have read that poem, and how delightfully it carries the breath of our River through the London smoke. Nor less welcome are the two poems on spring, the "Invitation to the Country," and the "Reply." In these, besides their verbal beauty and their charming pictures, is a manly philosophy of Life, which animates Mr. Bridges's more important pieces—his "Prometheus the Firebringer," and his "Nero," a tragedy remarkable for the representation of Nero himself, the luxurious human tiger. From "Prometheus" I make a short extract, to show the quality of Mr. Bridges's blank verse:

"Nor is there any spirit on earth astir,
Nor 'neath the airy vault, nor yet beyond
In any dweller in far-reaching space
Nobler or dearer than the spirit of man:
That spirit which lives in each and will not die,
That wooeth beauty, and for all good things
Urgeth a voice, or still in passion sigheth,
And where he loveth, draweth the heart with him."

Mr. Bridges's latest book is his "Eros and Psyche" (Bell & Sons, who publish the "Prometheus"). It is the old story very closely followed, and beautifully retold, with a hundred memories of ancient poets: Homer, Dante, Theocritus, as well as of Apuleius.

I have named Mr. Bridges here because his poems are probably all but unknown to readers well acquainted with many other English writers of late days. On them, especially on actual contemporaries or juniors in age, it would be almost impertinent for me to speak to you; but, even at that risk, I take the chance of directing you to the poetry of Mr. Bridges. I owe so much pleasure to its delicate air, that, if speech be impertinence, silence were ingratitude. {2}

FIELDING

To Mrs. Goodhart, in the Upper Mississippi Valley.

Dear Madam,—Many thanks for the New York newspaper you have kindly sent me, with the statistics of book-buying in the Upper Mississippi Valley. Those are interesting particulars which tell one so much about the taste of a community.

So the Rev. E. P. Roe is your favourite novelist there; a thousand of his books are sold for every two copies of the works of Henry Fielding? This appears to me to speak but oddly for taste in the Upper Mississippi Valley. On Mr. Roe's works I have no criticism to pass, for I have not read them carefully.

But I do think your neighbours lose a great deal by neglecting Henry Fielding. You will tell me he is coarse (which I cannot deny); you will remind me of what Dr. Johnson said, rebuking Mrs. Hannah More. "I never saw Johnson really angry with me but once," writes that sainted maiden lady. "I alluded to some witty passage in 'Tom Jones.'" He replied: "I am shocked to hear you quote from so vicious a book. I am sorry to hear you have read it; a confession which no modest lady should ever make."

You remind me of this, and that Johnson was no prude, and that his age was tolerant. You add that the literary taste of the Upper Mississippi Valley is much more pure than the waters of her majestic river, and that you only wish you knew who the two culprits were that bought books of Fielding's.

Ah, madam, how shall I answer you? Remember that if you have Johnson on your side, on mine I have Mrs. More herself, a character purer than "the consecrated snow that lies on Dian's lap." Again, we cannot believe Johnson was fair to Fielding, who had made his friend, the author of "Pamela," very uncomfortable by his jests. Johnson owned that he read all "Amelia" at one sitting. Could so worthy a man have been so absorbed by an unworthy book?

Once more, I am not recommending Fielding to boys and girls. "Tom Jones" was one of the works that Lydia Languish hid under the sofa; even Miss Languish did not care to be caught with that humorous foundling. "Fielding was the last of our writers who drew a man," Mr. Thackeray said, "and he certainly did not study from a draped model."

For these reasons, and because his language is often unpolished, and because his morality (that he is always preaching) is not for "those that eddy round and round," I do not desire to see Fielding popular among Miss Alcott's readers. But no man who cares for books can neglect him, and many women are quite manly enough, have good sense and good taste enough, to benefit by "Amelia," by much of "Tom Jones." I don't say by "Joseph Andrews." No man ever respected your sex more than Henry Fielding. What says his reformed rake, Mr. Wilson, in "Joseph Andrews"?

"To say the Truth, I do not perceive that Inferiority of Understanding which the Levity of Rakes, the Dulness of Men of Business, and the Austerity of the Learned would persuade us of in Women. As for my Wife, I declare I have found none of my own Sex capable of making juster Observations on Life, or of delivering them more agreeably, nor do I believe any one possessed of a faithfuller or braver Friend."

He has no other voice wherein to speak of a happy marriage. Can you find among our genteel writers of this age, a figure more beautiful, tender, devoted, and in all good ways womanly than Sophia Western's? "Yes," you will say; "but the man must have been a brute who could give her to Tom Jones, to 'that fellow who sold himself,' as Colonel Newcome said." "There you have me at an avail," in the language of the old romancers. There we touch the centre of Fielding's morality, a subject ill to discuss, a morality not for everyday preaching.

Fielding distinctly takes himself for a moralist. He preaches as continually as Thackeray. And his moral is this: "Let a man be kind, generous, charitable, tolerant, brave, honest—and we may pardon him vices of young blood, and the stains of adventurous living." Fielding has no mercy on a seducer. Lovelace would have fared worse with him than with Richardson, who, I verily believe, admired that infernal (excuse me) coward and villain. The case of young Nightingale, in "Tom Jones," will show you what Fielding thought of such gallants. Why, Tom himself preaches to Nightingale. "Miss Nancy's Interest alone, and not yours, ought to be your sole Consideration," cried Thomas, . . . "and the very best and truest Honour, which is Goodness, requires it of you," that is, requires that Nightingale shall marry Miss Nancy.

How Tom Jones combined these sentiments, which were perfectly honest, with his own astonishing lack of *retenue*, and with Lady Bellaston, is just the puzzle. We cannot very well argue about it. I only ask you to let Jones in his right mind partly excuse Jones in a number of very delicate situations. If you ask me whether Sophia had not, after her marriage, to be as forgiving as Amelia, I fear I must admit that probably it was so. But Dr. Johnson himself thought little of that.

I am afraid our only way of dealing with Fielding's morality is to take the best of it and leave the remainder alone. Here I find that I have unconsciously agreed with that well-known philosopher, Mr. James Boswell, the younger, of Auchinleck:

"The moral tendency of Fielding's writings . . . is ever favourable to honour and honesty, and cherishes the benevolent and generous affections. He who is as good as Fielding would make him is an amiable member of society, and may be led on by more regulated instructions to a higher state of ethical perfection."

Let us be as good and simple as Adams, without his vanity and his oddity, as brave and generous as Jones, without Jones's faults, and what a world of men and women it will become! Fielding did not paint that unborn world, he sketched the world he knew very well. He found that respectable people were often perfectly blind to the duties of charity in every sense of the word. He found that the only man in a whole company who pitied Joseph Andrews, when stripped and beaten by robbers was a postilion with defects in his moral character. In short, he knew that respectability often practised none but the strictly self-regarding virtues, and that poverty and recklessness did not always extinguish a native goodness of heart. Perhaps this discovery made him leniently disposed to "characters and situations so wretchedly low and dirty, that I," say the author of "Pamela," "could not be interested for any one of them."

How amusing Richardson always was about Fielding! How jealousy, spite, and the confusion of mind that befogs a prig when he is not taken seriously, do darken the eyes of the author of "those deplorably tedious lamentations, 'Clarissa' and 'Sir Charles Grandison,'" as Horace Walpole calls them!

Fielding asks his Muse to give him "humour and good humour." What novelist was ever so rich in both? Who ever laughed at mankind with so much affection for mankind in his heart? This love shines in every book of his. The poor have all his good-will, and in him an untired advocate and friend. What a life the poor led in the England of 1742! There never before was such tyranny without a servile insurrection. I remember a dreadful passage in "Joseph Andrews," where Lady Booby is trying to have Fanny, Joseph's sweetheart, locked up in prison:—

"It would do a Man good," says her accomplice, Scout, "to see his Worship, our Justice, commit a Fellow to *Bridewell*; he takes so much pleasure in it. And when once we ha' 'um there, we seldom hear any more o' 'um. He's either starved or eat up by Vermin in a Month's Time."

This England, with its dominant Squires, who behaved much like robber barons on the Rhine, was the merry England Fielding tried to turn from some of its ways. I seriously do believe that, with all its faults, it was a better place, with a better breed of men, than our England of to-day. But Fielding satirized intolerable injustice.

He would be a Reformer, a didactic writer. If we are to have nothing but "Art for Art's sake," that burly body of Harry Fielding's must even go to the wall. The first Beau Didapper of a critic that passes can shove him aside. He preaches like Thackeray; he writes "with a purpose" like Dickens—obsolete old authors. His cause is judged, and into Bridewell he goes, if *l'Art pour l'Art* is all the literary law and the prophets.

But Fielding cannot be kept in prison long. His noble English, his sonorous voice must be heard. There is somewhat inexpressibly heartening, to me, in the style of Fielding. One seems to be carried along, like a swimmer in a strong, clear stream, trusting one's self to every whirl and eddy, with a feeling of safety, of comfort, of delightful ease in the motion of the elastic water. He is a scholar, nay more, as Adams had his innocent vanity, Fielding has his innocent pedantry. He likes to quote Greek (fancy quoting Greek in a novel of to-day!) and to make the rogues of printers set it up correctly. He likes to air his ideas on Homer, to bring in a piece of Aristotle—not hackneyed—to show you that if he is writing about "characters and situations so wretchedly low and dirty," he is yet a student and a critic.

Mr. Samuel Richardson, a man of little reading, according to Johnson, was, I doubt, sadly put to it to understand Booth's conversations with the author who remarked that "Perhaps Mr. Pope followed the French Translations. I observe, indeed, he talks much in the Notes of Madame Dacier and Monsieur Eustathius." What knew Samuel of Eustathius? I not only can forgive Fielding his pedantry; I like it! I like a man of letters to be a scholar, and his little pardonable display and ostentation of his Greek only brings him nearer to us, who have none of his genius, and do not approach him but in his faults. They make him more human; one loves him for them as he loves Squire Western, with all his failings. Delightful, immortal Squire!

It was not he, it was another Tory Squire that called out "Hurray for old England! Twenty thousand honest Frenchmen are landed in Sussex." But it *was* Western that talked of "One Acton, that the Story Book says was turned into a Hare, and his own Dogs kill'd 'un, and eat 'un." And have you forgotten the popular discussion (during the Forty-five) of the affairs of the Nation, which, as Squire Western said, "all of us understand"? Said the Puppet-Man, "I don't care what Religion comes, provided the Presbyterians are not uppermost, for they are enemies to Puppet-Shows." But the Puppet-Man had no vote in 1745. Now, to our comfort, he can and does exercise the glorious privilege of the franchise.

There is no room in this epistle for Fielding's glorious gallery of characters—for Lady Bellaston, who remains a lady in her debaucheries, and is therefore so unlike our modern representative of her class, Lady Betty, in Miss Broughton's "Doctor Cupid;" for Square, and Thwackum, and Trulliber, and the jealous spite of Lady Booby, and Honour, that undying lady's maid, and Partridge, and Captain Blifil and Amelia, the fair and kind and good!

It is like the whole world of that old England—the maids of the Inn, the parish clerk, the two sportsmen, the hosts of the taverns, the beaux, the starveling authors—all alive; all (save the authors) full of beef and beer; a cudgel in every fist, every man ready for a brotherly bout at fisticuffs. What has become of it, the lusty old militant world? What will become of us, and why do we prefer to Fielding—a number of meritorious moderns? Who knows? But do not let *us* prefer anything to our English follower of Cervantes, our wise, merry, learned Sancho, trudging on English roads, like Don Quixote on the paths of Spain.

But I cannot convert you. You will turn to some story about store-clerks and summer visitors. Such is his fate who argues with the fair.

LONGFELLOW

To Walter Mainwaring, Esq., Lothian College, Oxford.

My dear Mainwaring,—You are very good to ask me to come up and listen to a discussion, by the College Browning Society, of the minor characters in "Sordello;" but I think it would suit me better, if you didn't mind, to come up when the May races are on. I am not deeply concerned about the minor characters in "Sordello," and have long reconciled myself to the conviction that I must pass through this pilgrimage without hearing Sordello's story told in an intelligible manner. Your letter, however, set me a-voyaging about my bookshelves, taking up a volume of poetry here and there.

What an interesting tract might be written by any one who could remember, and honestly describe, the impressions that the same books have made on him at different ages! There is Longfellow, for example. I have not read much in him for twenty years. I take him up to-day, and what a flood of memories his music brings with it! To me it is like a sad autumn wind blowing over the woods, blowing over the empty fields, bringing the scents of October, the song of a belated bird, and here and there a red leaf from the tree. There is that autumnal sense of things fair and far behind, in his poetry, or, if it is not there, his poetry stirs it in our forsaken lodges of the past. Yes, it comes to one out of one's boyhood; it breathes of a world very vaguely realized—a world of imitative sentiments and forebodings of hours to come. Perhaps Longfellow first woke me to that later sense of what poetry means, which comes with early manhood.

Before, one had been content, I am still content, with Scott in his battle pieces; with the ballads of the Border. Longfellow had a touch of reflection you do not find, of course, in battle poems, in a boy's favourites, such as "Of Nelson and the North," or "Ye Mariners of England."

His moral reflections may seem obvious now, and trite; they were neither when one was fifteen. To read the "Voices of the Night," in particular— those early pieces—is to be back at school again, on a Sunday, reading all alone on a summer's day, high in some tree, with a wide prospect of gardens and fields.

There is that mysterious note in the tone and measure which one first found in Longfellow, which has since reached our ears more richly and fully in Keats, in Coleridge, in Tennyson. Take, for example,

> "The welcome, the thrice prayed for, the most fair,
> The best-beloved Night!"

Is not that version of Euripides exquisite—does it not seem exquisite still, though this is not the quality you expect chiefly from Longfellow, though you rather look to him for honest human matter than for an indefinable beauty of manner?

I believe it is the manner, after all, of the "Psalm of Life" that has made it so strangely popular. People tell us, excellent people, that it is "as good as a sermon," that they value it for this reason, that its lesson has strengthened the hearts of men in our difficult life. They say so, and they think so: but the poem is not nearly as good as a sermon; it is not even coherent. But it really has an original cadence of its own, with its double rhymes; and the pleasure of this cadence has combined, with a belief that they are being edified, to make readers out of number consider the "Psalms of Life" a masterpiece. You—my learned prosodist and student of Browning and Shelley—will agree with me that it is *not* a masterpiece. But I doubt if you have enough of the experience brought by years to tolerate the opposite opinion, as your elders can.

How many other poems of Longfellow's there are that remind us of youth, and of those kind, vanished faces which were around us when we read "The Reaper and the Flowers"! I read again, and, as the poet says,

> "Then the forms of the departed
>   Enter at the open door,
> The belovèd, the true-hearted
>   Come to visit me once more."

Compare that simple strain, you lover of Théophile Gautier, with Théo's own "Château de Souvenir" in "Emaux et Camées," and confess the truth, which poet brings the break into the reader's voice? It is not the dainty, accomplished Frenchman, the jeweller in words; it is the simpler speaker of our English tongue who stirs you as a ballad moves you. I find one comes back to Longfellow, and to one's old self of the old years. I don't know a poem "of the affections," as Sir Barnes Newcome would have called it, that I like better than Thackeray's "Cane-bottomed Chair." Well, "The Fire of Driftwood" and this other of Longfellow's with its absolute lack of pretence, its artful avoidance of art, is not less tender and true.

> "And she sits and gazes at me
>   With those deep and tender eyes,
> Like the stars, so still and saintlike,
>   Looking downward from the skies."

It is from the skies that they look down, those eyes which once read the "Voices of the Night" from the same book with us, how long ago! So long ago that one was half-frightened by the legend of the "Beleaguered City." I know the ballad brought the scene to me so vividly that I expected, any frosty night, to see how

> "The white pavilions rose and fell
>   On the alarmed air;"

and it was down the valley of Ettrick, beneath the dark "Three Brethren's Cairn," that I half-hoped to watch when "the troubled army fled"—fled with battered banners of mist drifting through the pines, down to the Tweed and the sea. The "Skeleton in Armour" comes out once more as terrific as ever, and the "Wreck of the Hesperus" touches one in the old, simple way after so many, many days of verse-reading and even verse-writing.

In brief, Longfellow's qualities are so mixed with what the reader brings, with so many kindliest associations of memory, that one cannot easily criticize him in cold blood. Even in spite of this friendliness and affection which Longfellow wins, I can see, of course, that he does moralize too much. The first part of his lyrics is always the best; the part where he is dealing directly with his subject. Then comes the "practical application" as preachers say, and I feel now that it is sometimes uncalled for, disenchanting, and even manufactured.

Look at his "Endymion." It is the earlier verses that win you:

> "And silver white the river gleams
> As if Diana in her dreams
>   Had dropt her silver bow
>   Upon the meadows low."

That is as good as Ronsard, and very like him in manner and matter. But the moral and consolatory *application* is too long—too much dwelt on:

> "Like Dian's kiss, unasked, unsought,
> Love gives itself, but is not bought."

Excellent; but there are four weak, moralizing stanzas at the close, and not only does the poet "moralize his song," but the moral is feeble, and fantastic, and untrue. There are, though he denies it, myriads of persons now of whom it cannot be said that

> "Some heart, though unknown,
>   Responds unto his own."

If it were true, the reflection could only console a school-girl.

A poem like "My Lost Youth" is needed to remind one of what the author really was, "simple, sensuous, passionate." What a lovely verse this is, a verse somehow inspired by the breath of Longfellow's favourite Finnish

"Kalevala," "a verse of a Lapland song," like a wind over pines and salt coasts:

> "I remember the black wharves and the slips,
>   And the sea-tide, tossing free,
> And Spanish sailors with bearded lips,
> And the beauty and the mystery of the ships,
>   And the magic of the sea."

Thus Longfellow, though not a very great magician and master of language—not a Keats by any means—has often, by sheer force of plain sincerity, struck exactly the right note, and matched his thought with music that haunts us and will not be forgotten:

> "Ye open the eastern windows,
>   That look towards the sun,
> Where thoughts are singing swallows,
>   And the brooks of morning run."

There is a picture of Sandro Botticelli's, the Virgin seated with the Child by a hedge of roses, in a faint blue air, as of dawn in Paradise. This poem of Longfellow's, "The Children's Hour," seems, like Botticelli's painting, to open a door into the paradise of children, where their angels do ever behold that which is hidden from men—what no man hath seen at any time.

Longfellow is exactly the antithesis of Poe, who, with all his science of verse and ghostly skill, has no humanity, or puts none of it into his lines. One is the poet of Life, and everyday life; the other is the poet of Death, and of *bizarre* shapes of death, from which Heaven deliver us!

Neither of them shows any sign of being particularly American, though Longfellow, in "Evangeline" and "Hiawatha," and the "New England Tragedies," sought his topics in the history and traditions of the New World.

To me "Hiawatha" seems by far the best of his longer efforts; it is quite full of sympathy with men and women, nature, beasts, birds, weather, and wind and snow. Everything lives with a human breath, as everything should live in a poem concerned with these wild folk, to whom all the world, and all in it, is personal as themselves. Of course there are lapses of style in so long a piece. It jars on us in the lay of the mystic Chibiabos, the boy Persephone of the Indian Eleusinia, to be told that

> "the gentle Chibiabos
> *Sang in tones of deep emotion*!"

"Tones of deep emotion" may pass in a novel, but not in this epic of the wild wood and the wild kindreds, an epic in all ways a worthy record of those dim, mournful races which have left no story of their own, only here and there a ruined wigwam beneath the forest leaves.

A poet's life is no affair, perhaps, of ours. Who does not wish he knew as little of Burn's as of Shakespeare's? Of Longfellow's there is nothing to know but good, and his poetry testifies to it—his poetry, the voice of the kindest and gentlest heart that poet ever bore. I think there are not many things in poets' lives more touching than his silence, in verse, as to his own chief sorrow. A stranger intermeddles not with it, and he kept secret his brief lay on that insuperable and incommunicable regret. Much would have been lost had all poets been as reticent, yet one likes him better for it than if he had given us a new "Vita Nuova."

What an immense long way I have wandered from "Sordello," my dear Mainwaring, but when a man turns to his books, his thoughts, like those of a boy, "are long, long thoughts." I have not written on Longfellow's sonnets, for even you, impeccable sonneteer, admit that you admire them as much as I do.

A FRIEND OF KEATS

To Thomas Egerton, Esq., Lothian College, Oxford.

Dear Egerton,—Yes, as you say, Mr. Sidney Colvin's new "Life of Keats" {3} has only one fault, it's too short. Perhaps, also, it is almost too studiously free from enthusiasm. But when one considers how Keats (like Shelley) has been gushed about, and how easy it is to gush about Keats, one can only thank Mr. Colvin for his example of reserve. What a good fellow Keats was! How really manly and, in the best sense, moral he seems, when one compares his life and his letters with the vagaries of contemporary poets who lived longer than he, though they, too, died young, and who left more work, though not better, never so good, perhaps, as Keats's best.

However, it was not of Keats that I wished to write, but of his friend, John Hamilton Reynolds. *Noscitur a sociis*—a man is known by the company he keeps. Reynolds, I think, must have been excellent company, if we may judge him by his writings. He comes into Lord Houghton's "Life and Letters of Keats" very early (vol. i. p. 30). We find the poet writing to him in the April of 1817, from the Isle of Wight. "I shall forthwith begin my 'Endymion,' which I hope I shall have got some way with before you come, when we will read our verses in a delightful place I have set my heart upon, near the castle." Keats ends "your sincere friend," and a man to whom Keats was a sincere friend had some occasion for pride.

About Reynolds's life neither time nor space permits me to say very much, if I knew very much, which I don't. He was the son of a master in one of our large schools. He went to the Bar. He married a sister of Thomas Hood. He wrote, like Hood, in the *London Magazine*. With Hood for ally, he published "Odes and Addresses to Great People;" the third edition, which I have here, is of 1826. The late relations of the brothers-in-law were less happy; possibly the ladies of their families quarrelled; that is usually the way of the belligerent sex.

Reynolds died in the enjoyment of a judicial office in the Isle of Wight, some thirty years later than his famous friend, the author of "Endymion." "It is to be lamented," says Lord Houghton, "that Mr. Reynolds's own remarkable verse is not better known." Let us try to know it a little better.

I have not succeeded in getting Reynolds's first volume of poems, which was published before "Endymion." It contained some Oriental melodies, and won a careless good word from Byron. The earliest work of his I can lay my hand on is "The Fancy, a Selection from the Poetical Remains of the late Peter Corcoran, of Gray's Inn, Student at Law, with a brief memoir of his Life." There is a motto from Wordsworth:

"Frank are the sports, the stains are fugitive." {4}

It was the old palmy time of the Ring. Every one knows how Byron took lessons from Jackson the boxer; how Shelley had a fight at Eton in which he quoted Homer, but was licked by a smaller boy; how Christopher North whipped the professional pugilist; how Keats himself never had enough of fighting at school, and beat the butcher afterwards. His friend Reynolds, also, liked a set-to with the gloves. His imaginary character, Peter Corcoran, is a poetical lad, who becomes possessed by a passion for prize-fighting. It seems odd in a poet, but "the stains are fugitive."

We would liefer see a young man rejoicing in his strength and improving his science, than loafing about with long hair and giving anxious thought to the colour of his necktie. It is a disinterested preference, as fighting was never my *forte*, any more than it was Artemus Ward's. At school I was "more remarkable for what I suffered than for what I achieved."

Peter Corcoran "fought nearly as soon as he could walk," wherein he resembled Keats, and part of his character may even have been borrowed from the author of the "Ode to the Nightingale." Peter fell in love, wrote poetry, witnessed a "mill" at the Fives-Court, and became the Laureate of the Ring. "He has made a good set-to with Eales, Tom Belcher (the monarch of the *gloves!*), and Turner, and it is known that he has parried the difficult and ravaging hand even of Randall himself." "The difficult and ravaging hand"—there is a style for you!

Reynolds has himself the enthusiasm of his hero; let us remember that Homer, Virgil, and Theocritus have all described spirited rallies with admiration and good taste. From his dissipation in cider-cellars and coal-holes, this rival of Tom and Jerry wrote a sonnet that applies well enough to Reynolds's own career:

> "Were this a feather from an eagle's wing,
>   And thou, my tablet white! a marble tile
>   Taken from ancient Jove's majestic pile—
> And might I dip my feather in some spring,
> Adown Mount Ida threadlike wandering:—
>   And were my thoughts brought from some starry isle
>   In Heaven's blue sea—I then might with a smile
> Write down a hymn to fame, and proudly sing!
>
> "But I am mortal: and I cannot write
>   Aught that may foil the fatal wing of Time.
>   Silent, I look at Fame: I cannot climb

To where her Temple is—Not mine the might:—
   I have some glimmering of what is sublime—
But, ah! it is a most inconstant light."

Keats might have written this sonnet in a melancholy mood.

"About this time he (Peter) wrote a slang description of a fight he had witnessed to a lady." Unlucky Peter! "Was ever woman in this manner wooed?" The lady "glanced her eye over page after page in hopes of meeting with something that was intelligible," and no wonder she did not care for a long letter "devoted to the subject of a mill between Belasco and the Brummagem youth." Peter was so ill-advised as to appear before her with glorious scars, "two black eyes" in fact, and she "was inexorably cruel." Peter did not survive her disdain. "The lady still lives, and is married"! It is ever thus!

Peter's published works contain an American tragedy. Peter says he got it from a friend, who was sending him an American copy of "Guy Mannering" "to present to a young lady who, strange to say, read books and wore pockets," virtues unusual in the sex. One of the songs (on the delights of bull-baiting) contains the most vigorous lines I have ever met, but they are *too* vigorous for our lax age. The tragedy ends most tragically, and the moral comes in "better late," says the author, "than never." The other poems are all very lively, and very much out of date. Poor Peter!

Reynolds was married by 1818, and it is impossible to guess whether the poems of Peter Corcoran did or did not contain allusions to his own more lucky love affair. "Upon my soul," writes Keats, "I have been getting more and more close to you every day, ever since I knew you, and now one of the first pleasures I look to is your happy marriage." Reynolds was urging Keats to publish the "Pot of Basil" "as an answer to the attack made on me in *Blackwood's Magazine* and the *Quarterly Review.*"

Next Keats writes that he himself "never was in love, yet the voice and shape of a woman has haunted me these two days." On September 22, 1819, Keats sent Reynolds the "Ode to Autumn," than which there is no more perfect poem in the language of Shakespeare. This was the last of his published letters to Reynolds. He was dying, haunted eternally by that woman's shape and voice.

Reynolds's best-known book, if any of them can be said to be known at all, was published under the name of John Hamilton. It is "The Garden of Florence, and Other Poems" (Warren, London, 1821). There is a dedication—to his young wife.

"Thou hast entreated me to 'write no more,'" and he, as an elderly "man of twenty-four," promises to obey. "The lily and myself henceforth are *two*," he says, implying that he and the lily have previously been "one," a quaint confession from the poet of Peter Corcoran. There is something very pleasant in the graceful regret and obedience of this farewell to the Muse. He says to Mrs. Reynolds:

"I will not tell the world that thou hast chid
    My heart for worshipping the idol Muse;
That thy dark eye has given its gentle lid
    Tears for my wanderings; I may not choose
When thou dost speak but do as I am bid,—
    And therefore to the roses and the dews,
Very respectfully I make my bow;—
And turn my back upon the tulips now."

"The chief poems in the collection, taken from Boccaccio, were to have been associated with tales from the same source, intended to have been written by a friend; but illness on his part and distracting engagements on mine, prevented us from accomplishing our plan at the time; and Death now, to my deep sorrow, has frustrated it for ever!"

I cannot but quote what follows, the tribute to Keats's kindness, to the most endearing quality our nature possesses; the quality that was Scott's in such a winning degree, that was so marked in Molière,

"He, who is gone, was one of the very kindest friends I ever possessed, and yet he was not kinder, perhaps, to me than to others. His intense mind and powerful feeling would, I truly believe, have done the world some service had his life been spared—but he was of too sensitive a nature—and thus he was destroyed! One story he completed, and that is to me now the most pathetic poem in existence."

It was "Isabella, or the Pot of Basil."

The "Garden of Florence" is written in the couplets of "Endymion," and is a beautiful version of the tale once more retold by Alfred de Musset in "Simone." From "The Romance of Youth" let me quote one stanza, which applies to Keats:

"He read and dreamt of young Endymion,
    Till his romantic fancy drank its fill;
He saw that lovely shepherd sitting lone,
    Watching his white flocks upon Ida's hill;
The Moon adored him—and when all was still,
    And stars were wakeful—she would earthward stray,
And linger with her shepherd love, until
    The hooves of the steeds that bear the car of day,
Struck silver light in the east, and then she waned away!"

It was on Latmos, not Ida, that Endymion shepherded his flocks; but that is of no moment, except to schoolmasters. There are other stanzas of Reynolds worthy of Keats; for example, this on the Fairy Queen:

> "Her bodice was a pretty sight to see;
>   Ye who would know its colour,—be a thief
> Of the rose's muffled bud from off the tree;
>   And for your knowledge, strip it leaf by leaf
> Spite of your own remorse or Flora's grief,
>   Till ye have come unto its heart's pale hue;
> The last, last leaf, which is the queen,—the chief
>   Of beautiful dim blooms: ye shall not rue,
> At sight of that sweet leaf the mischief which ye do."

One does not know when to leave off gathering buds in the "Garden of Florence." Even after Shakespeare, and after Keats, this passage on wild flowers has its own charm:

> "We gathered wood flowers,—some blue as the vein
> O'er Hero's eyelid stealing, and some as white,
> In the clustering grass, as rich Europa's hand
> Nested amid the curls on Jupiter's forehead,
> What time he snatched her through the startled waves;—
> Some poppies, too, such as in Enna's meadows
> Forsook their own green homes and parent stalks,
> To kiss the fingers of Proserpina:
> And some were small as fairies' eyes, and bright
> As lovers' tears!"

I wish I had room for three or four sonnets, the Robin Hood sonnets to Keats, and another on a picture of a lady. Excuse the length of this letter, and read this:

> "Sorrow hath made thine eyes more dark and keen,
>   And set a whiter hue upon thy cheeks,—
>   And round thy pressèd lips drawn anguish-streaks,
> And made thy forehead fearfully serene.
> Even in thy steady hair her work is seen,
>   For its still parted darkness—till it breaks
>   In heavy curls upon thy shoulders—speaks
> Like the stern wave, how hard the storm hath been!
>
> "So looked that hapless lady of the South,
>   Sweet Isabella! at that dreary part
> Of all the passion'd hours of her youth;
>   When her green Basil pot by brother's art

Was stolen away; so look'd her painèd mouth
In the mute patience of a breaking heart!"

There let us leave him, the gay rhymer of prize-fighters and eminent persons—let us leave him in a serious hour, and with a memory of Keats. {5}

ON VIRGIL

To Lady Violet Lebas.

Dear Lady Violet,—Who can admire too much your undefeated resolution to admire only the right things? I wish I had this respect for authority! But let me confess that I have always admired the things which nature made me prefer, and that I have no power of accommodating my taste to the verdict of the critical. If I do not like an author, I leave him alone, however great his reputation. Thus I do not care for Mr. Gibbon, except in his Autobiography, nor for the elegant plays of M. Racine, nor very much for some of Wordsworth, though his genius is undeniable, nor excessively for the late Prof. Amiel. Why should we force ourselves into an affection for them, any more than into a relish for olives or claret, both of which excellent creatures I have the misfortune to dislike? No spectacle annoys me more than the sight of people who ask if it is "right" to take pleasure in this or that work of art. Their loves and hatreds will never be genuine, natural, spontaneous.

You say that it is "right" to like Virgil, and yet you admit that you admire the Mantuan, as the Scotch editor joked, "wi' deeficulty." I, too, must admit that my liking for much of Virgil's poetry is not enthusiastic, not like the admiration expressed, for example, by Mr. Frederic Myers, in whose "Classical Essays" you will find all that the advocates of the Latin singer can say for him. These heights I cannot reach, any more than I can equal that eloquence. Yet must Virgil always appear to us one of the most beautiful and moving figures in the whole of literature.

How sweet must have been that personality which can still win our affections, across eighteen hundred years of change, and through the mists of commentaries, and school-books, and traditions! Does it touch thee at all, oh gentle spirit and serene, that we, who never knew thee, love thee yet, and revere thee as a saint of heathendom? Have the dead any delight in the religion they inspire?

Id cinerem aut Manes credis curare sepultos?

I half fancy I can trace the origin of this personal affection for Virgil, which survives in me despite the lack of a very strong love of parts of his poems. When I was at school we met every morning for prayer, in a large circular hall, round which, on pedestals, were set copies of the portrait busts of great ancient writers. Among these was "the Ionian father of the rest," our father Homer, with a winning and venerable majesty. But the bust of Virgil was, I think, of white marble, not a cast (so, at least, I remember it), and was of a singular youthful purity and beauty, sharing my affections with a copy of the exquisite Psyche of Naples. It showed us that Virgil who was called "The Maiden" as Milton was named "The Lady of Christ's." I don't know the archeology of it, perhaps it was a mere work of modern fancy, but the charm of this image, beheld daily, overcame even the tedium of short scraps of the "Æneid" daily parsed, not without stripes and anguish. So I retain a sentiment for Virgil, though I well perceive the many drawbacks of his poetry.

It is not always poetry at first hand; it is often imitative, like all Latin poetry, of the Greek songs that sounded at the awakening of the world. This is more tolerable when Theocritus is the model, as in the "Eclogues," and less obvious in the "Georgics," when the poet is carried away into naturalness by the passion for his native land, by the longing for peace after cruel wars, by the joy of a country life. Virgil had that love of rivers which, I think, a poet is rarely without; and it did not need Greece to teach him to sing of the fields:

> *Propter aquam, tardis ingens ubi flexibus*
> *Mincius et tenera prætexit arundine ripas.*

"By the water-side, where mighty Mincius wanders, with links and loops, and fringes all the banks with the tender reed." Not the Muses of Greece, but his own *Casmenæ*, song-maidens of Italy, have inspired him here, and his music is blown through a reed of the Mincius. In many such places he shows a temper with which we of England, in our late age, may closely sympathize.

Do you remember that mediæval story of the building of Parthenope, how it was based, by the Magician Virgilius, on an egg, and how the city shakes when the frail foundation chances to be stirred? This too vast empire of ours is as frail in its foundation, and trembles at a word. So it was with the Empire of Rome in Virgil's time: civic revolution muttering within it, like the subterranean thunder, and the forces of destruction gathering without. In Virgil, as in Horace, you constantly note their anxiety, their apprehension for the tottering fabric of the Roman state. This it was, I think, and not the contemplation of human fortunes alone, that lent Virgil his melancholy. From these fears he looks for a shelter in the sylvan shades; he envies the ideal past of the golden world.

> *Aureus hanc vitam in terris Saturnus agebat!*

"Oh, for the fields! Oh, for Spercheius and Taygetus, where wander the Lacænian maids! Oh, that one would carry me to the cool valleys of Hæmus, and cover me with the wide shadow of the boughs! Happy was he who came to know the causes of things, who set his foot on fear and on inexorable Fate, and far below him heard the roaring of the streams of Hell! And happy he who knows the rural deities, Pan, and Sylvanus the Old, and the sisterhood of the nymphs! Unmoved is he by the people's favour, by the purple of kings, unmoved by all the perfidies of civil war, by the Dacian marching down from his hostile Danube; by the peril of the Roman state, and the Empire hurrying to its doom. He wasteth not his heart in pity of the poor, he envieth not the rich, he gathereth what fruits the branches bear and what the kindly wilderness unasked brings forth; he knows not our laws, nor the madness of the courts, nor the records of the common weal"—does not read the newspapers, in fact.

The sorrows of the poor, the luxury of the rich, the peril of the Empire, the shame and dread of each day's news, we too know them; like Virgil we too deplore them. We, in our reveries, long for some such careless paradise, but we place it not in Sparta but in the Islands of the Southern Seas. It is in passages of this temper that Virgil wins us most, when he speaks for himself and for his age, so distant, and so weary, and so modern; when his own thought, unborrowed and unforced, is wedded to the music of his own unsurpassable style.

But he does not always write for himself and out of his own thought, that style of his being far more frequently misapplied, wasted on telling a story that is only of feigned and foreign interest. Doubtless it was the "Æneid," his artificial and unfinished epic, that won Virgil the favour of the Middle Aces. To the Middle Ages, which knew not Greek, and knew not Homer, Virgil was the representative of the heroic and eternally interesting past. But to us who know Homer, Virgil's epic is indeed, "like moonlight unto sunlight;" is a beautiful empty world, where no real life stirs, a world that shines with a silver lustre not its own, but borrowed from "the sun of Greece."

Homer sang of what he knew, of spears and ships, of heroic chiefs and beggar men, of hunts and sieges, of mountains where the lion roamed, and of fairy isles where a goddess walked alone. He lived on the marches of the land of fable, when half the Mediterranean was a sea unsailed, when even Italy was as dimly descried as the City of the Sun in Elizabeth's reign. Of all that he knew he sang, but Virgil could only follow and imitate, with a pale antiquarian interest, the things that were alive for Homer. What could Virgil care for a tussle between two stout men-at-arms, for the clash of contending war-chariots, driven each on each, like wave against wave in the sea? All that tide had passed over, all the story of the "Æneid" is mere borrowed antiquity, like the Middle Ages of Sir Walter Scott; but the borrower had none of Scott's joy in the noise and motion of war, none of the Homeric "delight in battle."

Virgil, in writing the "Æneid," executed an imperial commission, and an ungrateful commission; it is the sublime of hack-work, and the legend may be true which declares that, on his death-bed, he wished his poem burned. He could only be himself here and there, as in that earliest picture of romantic love, as some have called the story of "Dido," not remembering, perhaps, that even here Virgil had before his mind a Greek model, that he was thinking of Apollonius Rhodius, and of Jason and Medea. He could be himself, too, in passages of reflection and description, as in the beautiful sixth book, with its picture of the under world, and its hints of mystical philosophy.

Could we choose our own heavens, there in that Elysian world might Virgil be well content to dwell, in the shadow of that fragrant laurel grove, with them who were "priests pure of life, while life was theirs, and holy singers, whose songs were worthy of Apollo." There he might muse on his own religion and on the Divinity that dwells in, that breathes in, that is, all things and more than all. Who could wish Virgil to be one of the spirits that

Lethæum ad flumen Dues evocat agmine magno,

that are called once more to the Lethean stream, and that once more, forgetful of their home, "into the world and wave of men depart?"

There will come no other Virgil, unless his soul, in accordance with his own philosophy, is among us to-day, crowned with years and honours, the singer of "Ulysses," of the "Lotus Eaters," of "Tithonus," and "Œnone."

So, after all, I have been enthusiastic, "maugre my head," as Malory says, and perhaps, Lady Violet, I have shown you why it is "right" to admire Virgil, and perhaps I have persuaded nobody but myself.

P.S.—Mr. Coleridge was no great lover of Virgil, inconsistently. "If you take from Virgil his diction and metre, what do you leave him?" Yet Mr. Coleridge had defined poetry as "the *best* words, in the best order"—that is, "diction and metre." He, therefore, proposed to take from Virgil his poetry, and then to ask what was left of the Poet!

AUCASSIN AND NICOLETTE

To the Lady Violet Lebas.

Dear Lady Violet,—I do not wonder that you are puzzled by the language of the first French novel. The French of "Aucassin et Nicolette" is not French after the school of Miss Pinkerton, at Chiswick. Indeed, as the little song-story has been translated into modern French by M. Bida, the painter (whose book is very scarce), I presume even the countrywomen of Aucassin find it difficult. You will not expect me to write an essay on the grammar, nor would you read it if I did. The chief thing is that "s" appears as the sign of the singular, instead of being the sign of the plural, and the nouns have cases.

The story must be as old as the end of the twelfth century, and must have received its present form in Picardy. It is written, as you see, in alternate snatches of verse and prose. The verse, which was chanted, is not rhymed as a rule, but each *laisse*, or screed, as in the "Chanson de Roland," runs on the same final assonance, or vowel sound throughout.

So much for the form. Who is the author? We do not know, and never shall know. Apparently he mentions himself in the first lines:

> "Who would listen to the lay,
> Of the captive old and gray;"

for this is as much sense as one can make out of *del deport du viel caitif.*

The author, then, was an old fellow. I think we might learn as much from the story. An old man he was, or a man who felt old. Do you know whom he reminds me of? Why, of Mr. Bowes, of the Theatre Royal, Chatteris; of Mr. Bowes, that battered, old, kindly sentimentalist who told his tale with Mr. Arthur Pendennis.

It is a love story, a story of love overmastering, without conscience or care of aught but the beloved. And the *viel caitif* tells it with sympathy, and with a smile. "Oh, folly of fondness," he seems to cry; "oh, pretty fever and foolish; oh, absurd happy days of desolation:

> *"When I was young, as you are young,*
> *And lutes were touched, and songs were sung!*
> *And love-lamps in the windows hung!"*

It is the very tone of Thackeray, when Thackeray is tender; and the world heard it first from this elderly nameless minstrel, strolling with his viol and his singing boys, a blameless D'Assoucy, from castle to castle in the happy poplar land. I think I see him and hear him in the silver twilight, in the court of some château of Picardy, while the ladies around sit listening on silken cushions, and their lovers, fettered with silver chains, lie at their feet. They listen, and look, and do not think of the minstrel with his gray head, and his green heart; but we think of him. It is an old man's work, and a weary man's work. You can easily tell the places where he has lingered and been pleased as he wrote.

The story is simple enough. Aucassin, son of Count Garin, of Beaucaire, loved so well fair Nicolette, the captive girl from an unknown land, that he would never be dubbed knight, nor follow tourneys; nor even fight against his father's mortal foe, Count Bougars de Valence. So Nicolette was imprisoned high in a painted chamber. But the enemy were storming the town, and, for the promise of "one word or two with Nicolette, and one kiss," Aucassin armed himself and led out his men. But he was all adream about Nicolette, and his horse bore him into the press of foes ere he knew it. Then he heard them contriving his death, and woke out of his dream.

"The damoiseau was tall and strong, and the horse whereon he sat fierce and great, and Aucassin laid hand to sword, and fell a-smiting to right and left, and smote through helm and headpiece, and arm and shoulder, making a murder about him, like a wild boar the hounds fall on in the forest. There slew he ten knights, and smote down seven, and mightily and knightly he hurled through the press, and charged home again, sword in hand." For that hour Aucassin struck like one of Mallory's men in the best of all romances. But though he took Count Bougars prisoner, his father would not keep his word, nor let him have one word or two with Nicolette, and one kiss. Nay, Aucassin was thrown into prison in an old tower. There he sang of Nicolette,

> "Was it not the other day
> That a pilgrim came this way?
> And a passion him possessed,
> That upon his bed he lay,
> Lay, and tossed, and knew no rest,
> In his pain discomforted.
> But thou camest by his bed,
> Holding high thine amice fine
> And thy kirtle of ermine.
> Then the beauty that is thine
> Did he look on; and it fell
> That the Pilgrim straight was well,
> Straight was hale and comforted.
> And he rose up from his bed,

And went back to his own place
Sound and strong, and fair of face."

Thus Aucassin makes a Legend of his lady, as it were, assigning to her beauty such miracles as faith attributes to the excellence of the saints.

Meanwhile, Nicolette had slipped from the window of her prison chamber, and let herself down into the garden, where she heard the song of the nightingales. "Then caught she up her kirtle in both hands, behind and before, and flitted over the dew that lay deep on the grass, and fled out of the garden, and the daisy flowers bending below her tread seemed dark against her feet, so white was the maiden." Can't you see her stealing with those "feet of ivory," like Bombyca's, down the dark side of the silent moonlit streets of Beaucaire?

Then she came where Aucassin was lamenting in his cell, and she whispered to him how she was fleeing for her life. And he answered that without her he must die; and then this foolish pair, in the very mouth of peril, must needs begin a war of words as to which loved the other best!

"Nay, fair sweet friend," saith Aucassin, "it may not be that thou lovest me more than I love thee. Woman may not love man as man loves woman, for a woman's love lies no deeper than in the glance of her eye, and the blossom of her breast, and her foot's tip-toe; but man's love is in his heart planted, whence never can it issue forth and pass away."

So while they speak

"In debate as birds are,
Hawk on bough,"

comes the kind sentinel to warn them of a danger. And Nicolette flees, and leaps into the fosse, and thence escapes into a great forest and lonely. In the morning she met shepherds merry over their meat, and bade them tell Aucassin to hunt in that forest, where he should find a deer whereof one glance would cure him of his malady. The shepherds are happy, laughing people, who half mock Nicolette, and quite mock Aucassin, when he comes that way. But at first they took Nicolette for a *fée*, such a beauty shone so brightly from her, and lit up all the forest. Aucassin they banter; and indeed the free talk of the peasants to their lord's son in that feudal age sounds curiously, and may well make us reconsider our notions of early feudalism.

But Aucassin learns at least that Nicolette is in the wood, and he rides at adventure after her, till the thorns have ruined his silken surcoat, and the blood, dripping from his torn body, makes a visible track in the grass. So, as he wept, he met a monstrous man of the wood, that asked him why he lamented. And he said he was sorrowing for a lily-white hound that he had lost. Then the wild man mocked him, and told his own tale. He was in that estate which Achilles, among the ghosts, preferred to all the kingship of the dead outworn. He was hind and hireling to a villein, and he had lost one of the villein's oxen. For that he dared not go into the town, where a prison awaited him. Moreover, they had dragged the very bed from under his old mother, to pay the price of the ox, and she lay on straw; and at that the woodman wept.

A curious touch, is it not, of pity for the people? The old poet is serious for one moment. "Compare," he says, "the sorrows of sentiment, of ladies and lovers, praised in song, with the sorrows of the poor, with troubles that are real and not of the heart!" Even Aucassin the lovelorn feels it, and gives the hind money to pay for his ox, and so riding on comes to a lodge that Nicolette has built with blossoms and boughs. And Aucassin crept in and looked through a gap in the fragrant walls of the lodge, and saw the stars in heaven, and one that was brighter than the rest.

Does one not feel it, the cool of that old summer night, the sweet smell of broken boughs and trodden grass and deep dew, and the shining of the star?

> "Star that I from far behold
> That the moon draws to her fold,
> Nicolette with thee doth dwell,
> My sweet love with locks of gold,"

sings Aucassin. "And when Nicolette heard Aucassin, right so came she unto him, and passed within the lodge, and cast her arms about his neck and kissed and embraced him:

> "Fair sweet friend, welcome be thou!"
> "And thou, fair sweet love, be thou welcome!"

There the story should end, in a dream of a summer's night. But the old minstrel did not end it so, or some one has continued his work with a heavier hand. Aucassin rides, he cares not whither, if he has but his love with him. And they come to a fantastic land of burlesque, such as Pantagruel's crew touched at many a time. And Nicolette is taken by Carthaginian pirates, and proves to be daughter to the King of Carthage, and leaves his court and comes to Beaucaire in the disguise of a ministrel, and "journeys end in lovers' meeting."

That is all the tale, with its gaps, its careless passages, its adventures that do not interest the poet. He only cares for youth, love, spring, flowers, and the song of the birds; the rest, except the passage about the hind, is mere "business" done casually, because the audience expects broad jests, hard blows, misadventures, recognitions. What lives is the touch of poetry, of longing, of tender heart, of humorous resignation. It lives, and always must live, "while the nature of man is the same." The poet hopes his tale will gladden sad men. This service it did for M. Bida, he says, in the dreadful year of 1870-71, when he translated "Aucassin." This, too, it has done for me in days not delightful. {6}

PLOTINUS (A.D. 200-262)

To the Lady Violet Lebas.

Dear Lady Violet,—You are discursive and desultory enough, as a reader, to have pleased even the late Lord Iddesleigh. It was "Aucassin and Nicolette" only a month ago, and to-day you have been reading Lord Lytton's "Strange Story," I am sure, for you want information about Plotinus! He was born (about A.D. 200) in Wolf-town (Lycopolis), in Egypt, the town, you know, where the natives might not eat wolves, poor fellows, just as the people of Thebes might not eat sheep. Probably this prohibition caused Plotinus no regret, for he was a consistent vegetarian.

However, we are advancing too rapidly, and we must discuss Plotinus more in order. His name is very dear to mystic novelists, like the author of "Zanoni." They always describe their favourite hero as "deep in Plotinus or Iamblichus," and I venture to think that nearly represents the depth of their own explorations. We do not know exactly when Plotinus was born. Like many ladies he used to wrap up his age in a mystery, observing that these petty details about the body (a mere husk of flesh binding the soul) were of no importance. He was not weaned till he was eight years old, a singular circumstance. Having a turn for philosophy, he attended the schools of Alexandria, concerning which Kingsley's "Hypatia" is the most accessible authority.

All these anecdotes, I should have said, we learn from Porphyry, the Tyrian, who was a kind of Boswell to Plotinus. The philosopher himself often reminds me of Dr. Johnson, especially as Dr. Johnson is described by Mr. Carlyle. Just as the good doctor was a sound Churchman in the beginning of the age of new ideas, so Plotinus was a sound pagan in the beginning of the triumph of Christianity.

Like Johnson, Plotinus was lazy and energetic and short-sighted. He wrote a very large number of treatises, but he never took the trouble to read through them when once they were written, because his eyes were weak. He was superstitious, like Dr. Johnson, yet he had lucid intervals of common sense, when he laughed at the superstitions of his disciples. Like Dr. Johnson, he was always begirt by disciples, men and women, Bozzys and Thrales. He was so full of honour and charity, that his house was crowded with persons in need of help and friendly care. Though he lived so much in the clouds and among philosophical abstractions, he was an excellent man of business. Though a philosopher he was pious, and was courageous, dreading the plague no more than the good doctor dreaded the tempest that fell on him when he was voyaging to Coll.

You will admit that the parallel is pretty close for an historical parallel, despite the differences between the ascetic of Wolf-town and the sage of Bolt Court, hard by Fleet Street!

To return to the education of Plotinus. He was twenty-eight when he went up to the University of Alexandria. For eleven years he diligently attended the lectures of Ammonius. Then he went on the Emperor Gordian's expedition to the East, hoping to learn the philosophy of the Hindus. The Upanishads would have puzzled Plotinus, had he reached India; but he never did. Gordian's army was defeated in Mesopotamia, no "blessed word" to Gordian, and Plotinus hardly escaped with his life. He must have felt like Stendhal on the retreat from Moscow.

From Syria his friend and disciple Amelius led him to Rome, and here, as novelists say, "a curious thing happened." There was in Rome an Egyptian priest, who offered to raise up the Demon, or Guardian Angel, of Plotinus in visible form. But there was only one pure spot in all Rome, so said the priest, and this spot was the Temple of Isis. Here the *séance* was held, and no demon appeared, but a regular God of one of the first circles. So terrified was an onlooker that he crushed to death the living birds which he held in his hands for some ritual or magical purpose.

It was a curious scene, a cosmopolitan confusion of Egypt, Rome, Isis, table-turning, the late Mr. Home, religion, and mummery, while Christian hymns of the early Church were being sung, perhaps in the garrets around, outside the Temple of Isis. The discovery that he had a god for his guardian angel gave Plotinus plenty of confidence in dealing with rival philosophers. For example, Alexandrinus Olympius, another mystic, tried magical arts against Plotinus. But Alexandrinus, suddenly doubling up during lecture with unaffected agony, cried, "Great virtue hath the soul of Plotinus, for my spells have returned against myself." As for Plotinus, he remarked among his disciples, "Now the body of Alexandrinus is collapsing like an empty purse."

How diverting it would be, Lady Violet, if our modern controversialists had those accomplishments, and if Mr. Max Müller could, literally, "double up" Professor Whitney, or if any one could cause Peppmüller to collapse with his queer Homeric theory! Plotinus had many such arts. A piece of jewellery was stolen from one of his *protégées*, a lady, and he detected the thief, a servant, by a glance. After being flogged within an inch of his life, the servant (perhaps to save the remaining inch) confessed all.

Once when Porphyry was at a distance, and was meditating suicide, Plotinus appeared at his side, saying, "This that thou schemest cometh not of the pure intellect, but of black humours," and so sent Porphyry for change of air to Sicily. This was thoroughly good advice, but during the absence of the disciple the master died.

Porphyry did not see the great snake that glided into the wall when Plotinus expired; he only heard of the circumstance. Plotinus's last words were: "I am striving to release that which is divine within us, and to merge it in the universally divine." It is a strange mixture of philosophy and savage survival. The Zulus still believe that the souls of the dead reappear, like the soul of Plotinus, in the form of serpents.

Plotinus wrote against the paganizing Christians, or Gnostics. Like all great men, he was accused of plagiarism. A defence of great men accused of literary theft would be as valuable as Naudé's work of a like name about magic. On his death the Delphic Oracle, in very second-rate hexameters, declared that Plotinus had become a demon.

Such was the life of Plotinus, a man of sense and virtue, and so modest that he would not allow his portrait to be painted. His character drew good men round him, his repute for supernatural virtues brought "fools into a circle." What he meant by his belief that four times he had, "whether in the body or out of the body," been united with the Spirit of the world, who knows? What does Tennyson mean when he writes:

> "So word by word, and line by line,
>   The dead man touch'd me from the past,
>   And all at once it seem'd at last
> His living soul was flashed on mine.
>
> And mine in his was wound and whirl'd
>   About empyreal heights of thought,
>   And came on that which is, and caught
> The deep pulsations of the world."

Mystery! We cannot fathom it; we know not the paths of the souls of Pascal and Gordon, of Plotinus and St. Paul. They are wise with a wisdom not of this world, or with a foolishness yet more wise.

In his practical philosophy Plotinus was an optimist, or at least he was at war with pessimism.

"They that love God bear lightly the ways of the world—bear lightly whatsoever befalls them of necessity in the general movement of things." He believed in a rest that remains for the people of God, "where they speak not one with the other; but, as we understand many things by the eyes only, so does soul read soul in heaven, where the spiritual body is pure, and nothing is hidden, and nothing feigned." The arguments by which these opinions are buttressed may be called metaphysical, and may be called worthless; the conviction, and the beauty of the language in which it is stated, remain immortal possessions.

Why such a man as Plotinus, with such ideas, remained a pagan, while Christianity offered him a sympathetic refuge, who can tell? Probably natural conservatism, in him as in Dr. Johnson—conservatism and taste—caused his adherence to the forms at least of the older creeds. There was much to laugh at in Plotinus, and much to like. But if you read him in hopes of material for strange stories, you will be disappointed. Perhaps Lord Lytton and others who have invoked his name in fiction (like Vivian Grey in Lord Beaconsfield's tale) knew his name better than his doctrine. His "Enneads," even as edited by his patient Boswell, Porphyry, are not very light subjects of study.

LUCRETIUS

To the Rev. Geoffrey Martin, Oxford.

Dear Martin,—"How individuals found religious consolation from the creeds of ancient Greece and Rome" is, as you quote C. O. Müller, "a very curious question." It is odd that while we have countless books on the philosophy and the mythology and the ritual of the classic peoples, we hear about their religion in the modern sense scarcely anything from anybody. We know very well what gods they worshipped, and what sacrifices they offered to the Olympians, and what stories they told about their deities, and about the beginnings of things. We know, too, in a general way, that the gods were interested in morality. They would all punish offences in their own department, at least when it was a case of *numine læso*, when the god who protected the hearth was offended by breach of hospitality, or when the gods invoked to witness an oath were offended by perjury.

But how did a religiously minded man regard the gods? What hope or what fears did he entertain with regard to the future life? Had he any sense of *sin*, as more than a thing that could be expiated by purification with the blood of slaughtered swine, or by purchasing the prayers and "masses," so to speak, of the mendicant clergy or charlatans, mentioned by Plato in the "Republic"? About these great questions of the religious life—the Future and man's fortunes in the future, the punishment or reward of justice or iniquity—we really know next to nothing.

That is one reason why the great poem of Lucretius seems so valuable to me. The *De Rerum Natura* was written for no other purpose than to destroy Religion, as Lucretius understood it, to free men's minds from all dread as to future punishment, all hope of Heaven, all dread or desire for the interference of the gods in this mortal life of ours on earth. For no other reason did Lucretius desire to "know the causes of things," except that the knowledge would bring "emancipation," as people call it, from the gods, to whom men had hitherto stood in the relation of the Roman son to the Roman sire, under the *patria potestas* or *in manu patris*.

As Lucretius wrought all his arduous work to this end, it follows that his fellow-countrymen *must* have gone in a constant terror about spiritual penalties, which we seldom associate in thought with the "blithe" and careless existence of the ancient peoples. In every line of Lucretius you read the joy and the indignation of the slave just escaped from an intolerable thraldom to fear. Nobody could well have believed on any other evidence that the classical people had a gloomy Calvinism of their own time. True, as early as Homer, we hear of the shadowy existence of the souls, and of the torments endured by the notably wicked; by impious ghosts, or tyrannical, like Sisyphus and Tantalus. But when we read the opening books of the "Republic," we find the educated friends of Socrates treating these terrors as old-wives' fables. They have heard, they say, that such notions circulate among the people, but they seem never for a moment to have themselves believed in a future of rewards and punishments.

The remains of ancient funereal art, in Etruria or Attica, usually show us the semblances of the dead lying at endless feasts, or receiving sacrifices of food and wine (as in Egypt) from their descendants, or, perhaps, welcoming the later dead, their friends who have just rejoined them. But it is only in the descriptions by Pausanias and others of certain old wall-paintings that we hear of the torments of the wicked, of the demons that torture them and, above all, of the great chief fiend, coloured like a carrion fly. To judge from Lucretius, although so little remains to us of this creed, yet it had a very strong hold of the minds of people, in the century before Christ. Perhaps the belief was reinforced by the teaching of Socrates, who, in the vision of Er, in the "Republic," brings back, in a myth, the old popular faith in a *Purgatorio*, if not in an *Inferno*.

In the "Phædo," for certain, we come to the very definite account of a Hell, a place of eternal punishment, as well as of a Purgatory, whence souls are freed when their sins are expiated. "The spirits beyond redemption, for the multitude of their murders or sacrileges, Fate hurls into Tartarus, whence they never any more come forth." But souls of lighter guilt abide a year in Tartarus, and then drift out down the streams Cocytus and Pyriphlegethon. Thence they reach the marsh of Acheron, but are not released until they have received the pardon of the souls whom in life they had injured.

All this, and much more to the same purpose in other dialogues of Plato's, appears to have been derived by Socrates from the popular unphilosophic traditions, from Folk-lore in short, and to have been raised by him to the rank of "pious opinion," if not of dogma. Now, Lucretius represents nothing but the reaction against all this dread of future doom, whether that dread was inculcated by Platonic philosophy or by popular belief. The latter must have been much the more powerful and widely diffused. It follows that the Romans, at least, must have been haunted by a constant dread of judgment to come, from which, but for the testimony of Lucretius and his manifest sincerity, we might have believed them free.

Perhaps we may regret the existence of this Roman religion, for it did its best to ruin a great poet. The sublimity of the language of Lucretius, when he can leave his attempts at scientific proof, the closeness of his observation, his enjoyment of life, of Nature, and his power of painting them, a certain largeness of touch, and noble amplitude of manner—these, with a burning sincerity, mark him above all others that smote the Latin lyre. Yet these great qualities are half-crushed by his task, by his attempt to turn the atomic theory into verse, by his unsympathetic effort to destroy all faith and hope, because these were united, in his mind, with dread of Styx and Acheron.

It is an almost intolerable philosophy, the philosophy of eternal sleep, without dreams and without awakening. This belief is wholly divorced from joy, which inspires all the best art. This negation of hope has "close-lipped Patience for its only friend."

In vain does Lucretius paint pictures of life and Nature so large, so glowing, so majestic that they remind us of nothing but the "Fête Champêtre" of Giorgione, in the Louvre. All that life is a thing we must leave soon, and forever, and must be hopelessly lapped in an eternity of blind silence. "I shall let men see the certain end of all," he cries; "then will they resist religion, and the threats of priests and prophets." But this "certain end" is exactly what mortals do not desire to see. To this sleep they prefer even *tenebras Orci, vastasque lacunas.*

They will not be deprived of gods, "the friends of man, merciful gods, compassionate." They will not turn from even a faint hope in those to the Lucretian deities in their endless and indifferent repose and divine "delight in immortal and peaceful life, far, far away from us and ours—life painless and fearless, needing nothing we can give, replete with its own wealth, unmoved by prayer and promise, untouched by anger."

Do you remember that hymn, as one may call it, of Lucretius to Death, to Death which does not harm us. "For as we knew no hurt of old, in ages when the Carthaginian thronged against us in war, and the world was shaken with the shock of fight, and dubious hung the empire over all things mortal by sea and land, even so careless, so unmoved, shall we remain, in days when we shall no more exist, when the bond of body and soul that makes our life is broken. Then naught shall move us, nor wake a single sense, not though earth with sea be mingled, and sea with sky." There is no hell, he cries, or, like Omar, he says, "Hell is the vision of a soul on fire."

Your true Tityus, gnawed by the vulture, is only the slave of passion and of love; your true Sisyphus (like Lord Salisbury in *Punch*) is only the politician, striving always, never attaining; the stone rolls down again from the hill-crest, and thunders far along the plain.

Thus his philosophy, which gives him such a delightful sense of freedom, is rejected after all these years of trial by men. They feel that since those remotest days

"Quum Venus in silvis jungebat corpora amantum,"

they have travelled the long, the weary way Lucretius describes to little avail, if they may not keep their hopes and fears. Robbed of these we are robbed of all; it serves us nothing to have conquered the soil and fought the winds and waves, to have built cities, and tamed fire, if the world is to be "dispeopled of its dreams." Better were the old life we started from, and dreams therewith, better the free days—

"Novitas tum florida mundi
Pabula dia tulit, miseris mortablibus ampla;"

than wealth or power, and neither hope nor fear, but one certain end of all before the eyes of all.

Thus the heart of man has answered, and will answer Lucretius, the noblest Roman poet, and the least beloved, who sought, at last, by his own hand, they say, the doom that Virgil waited for in the season appointed.

TO A YOUNG AMERICAN BOOK-HUNTER

To Philip Dodsworth, Esq., New York.

Dear Dodsworth,—Let me congratulate you on having joined the army of book-hunters. "Everywhere have I sought peace and found it nowhere," says the blessed Thomas à Kempis, "save in a corner with a book." Whether that good monk wrote the "De Imitatione Christi" or not, one always likes him for his love of books. Perhaps he was the only book-hunter that ever wrought a miracle. "Other signs and miracles which he was wont to tell as having happened at the prayer of an unnamed person, are believed to have been granted to his own, such as the sudden reappearance of a lost book in his cell." Ah, if Faith, that moveth mountains, could only bring back the books we have lost, the books that have been borrowed from us! But we are a faithless generation.

From a collector so much older and better experienced in misfortune than yourself, you ask for some advice on the sport of book-hunting. Well, I will give it; but you will not take it. No; you will hunt wild, like young pointers before they are properly broken.

Let me suppose that you are "to middle fortune born," and that you cannot stroll into the great book-marts and give your orders freely for all that is rich and rare. You are obliged to wait and watch an opportunity, to practise that maxim of the Stoic's, "Endure and abstain." Then abstain from rushing at every volume, however out of the line of your literary interests, which seems to be a bargain. Probably it is not even a bargain; it can seldom be cheap to you, if you do not need it, and do not mean to read it.

Not that any collector reads all his books. I may have, and indeed do possess, an Aldine Homer and Caliergus his Theocritus; but I prefer to study the authors in a cheap German edition. The old editions we buy mainly for their beauty, and the sentiment of their antiquity and their associations.

But I don't take my own advice. The shelves are crowded with books quite out of my line—a whole small library of tomes on the pastime of curling, and I don't curl; and "God's Revenge against Murther," though (so far) I am not an assassin. Probably it was for love of Sir Walter Scott, and his mention of this truculent treatise, that I purchased it. The full title of it is "The Triumphs of God's Revenge against the Crying and Execrable Sinne of (willful and premeditated) Murther." Or rather there is nearly a column more of title, which I spare you. But the pictures are so bad as to be nearly worth the price. Do not waste your money, like your foolish adviser, on books like that, or on "Les Sept Visions de Don Francisco de Quevedo," published at Cologne, in 1682.

Why in the world did I purchase this, with the title-page showing Quevedo asleep, and all his seven visions floating round him in little circles like soap-bubbles? Probably because the book was published by Clement Malassis, and perhaps he was a forefather of that whimsical Frenchman, Poulet Malassis, who published for Banville, and Baudelaire, and Charles Asselineau. It was a bad reason. More likely the mere cheapness attracted me.

Curiosity, not cheapness, assuredly, betrayed me into another purchase. If I want to read "The Pilgrim's Progress," of course I read it in John Bunyan's good English. Then why must I ruin myself to acquire "Voyage d'un Chrestien vers l'Eternité. Ecrit en Anglois, par Monsieur Bunjan, F.M., en Bedtfort, et nouvellement traduit en François. Avec Figures. A Amsterdam, chez Jean Boekholt Libraire près de la Bourse, 1685"? I suppose this is the oldest French version of the famed allegory. Do you know an older? Bunyan was still living and, indeed, had just published the second part of the book, about Christian's wife and children, and the deplorable young woman whose name was Dull.

As the little volume, the Elzevir size, is bound in blue morocco, by Cuzin, I hope it is not wholly a foolish bargain; but what do I want, after all, with a French "Pilgrim's Progress"? These are the errors a man is always making who does not collect books with system, with a conscience and an aim.

Do have a specially. Make a collection of works on few subjects, well chosen. And what subjects shall they be? That depends on taste. Probably it is well to avoid the latest fashion. For example, the illustrated French books of the eighteenth century are, at this moment, *en hausse*. There is a "boom" in them. Fifty years ago Brunet, the author of the great "Manuel," sneered at them. But, in his, "Library Companion," Dr. Dibdin, admitted their merit. The illustrations by Gravelot, Moreau, Marillier, and the rest, are certainly delicate, graceful, full of character, stamped with style. But only the proofs before letters are very much valued, and for these wild prices are given by competitive millionaires. You cannot compete with them.

It is better wholly to turn the back on these books and on any others at the height of the fashion, unless you meet them for fourpence on a stall. Even then should a gentleman take advantage of a poor bookseller's ignorance? I don't know. I never fell into the temptation, because I never was tempted. Bargains, real bargains, are so rare that you may hunt for a lifetime and never meet one.

The best plan for a man who has to see that his collection is worth what it cost him, is probably to confine one's self to a single line, say, in your case, first editions of new English, French, and American books that are likely to rise in value. I would try, were I you, to collect first editions of Longfellow, Bryant, Whittier, Poe, and Hawthorne.

As to Poe, you probably will never have a chance. Outside of the British Museum, where they have the "Tamerlane" of 1827, I have only seen one early example of Poe's poems. It is "Al Aaraaf, Tamerlane, and Minor Poems, by Edgar A. Poe. Baltimore: Hatch and Dunning, 1829, 8vo, pp. 71." The book "came to Mr. Locker (Mr. Frederick Locker-Lampson), through Mr. R. H. Stoddard, the American poet." So says Mr. Locker-Lampson's Catalogue. He also has the New York edition of 1831.

These books are extraordinarily rare; you are more likely to find them in some collection of twopenny rubbish than to buy them in the regular market. Bryant's "Poems" (Cambridge, 1821) must also be very rare, and Emerson's of 1847, and Dr. Oliver Wendell Holmes's of 1836, and Longfellow's "Voices of the Night," 1839, and Mr. Lowell's "A Year's Life;" none of these can be common, and all are desirable, as are Mr. Whittier's "Legends of New England" (1831), and "Poems" (1838).

Perhaps you may never be lucky enough to come across them cheap; no doubt they are greatly sought for by amateurs. Indeed, all American books of a certain age or of a special interest are exorbitantly dear. Men like Mr. James Lenox used to keep the market up. One cannot get the Jesuit "Relations"—shabby little missionary reports from Canada, in dirty vellum.

Cartier, Perrot, Champlain, and the other early explorers' books are beyond the means of a working student who needs them. May *you* come across them in a garret of a farmhouse, or in some dusty lane of the city. Why are they not reprinted, as Mr. Arber has reprinted "Captain John Smith's Voyages, and Reports on Virginia"? The very reprints, when they have been made, are rare and hard to come by.

There are certain modern books, new books, that "go up" rapidly in value and interest. Mr. Swinburne's "Atalanta" of 1865, the quarto in white cloth, is valued at twenty dollars. Twenty years ago one dollar would have purchased it. Mr. Austin Dobson's "Proverbs in Porcelain" is also in demand among the curious. Nay, even I may say about the first edition of "Ballades in Blue China" (1880), as Gibbon said of his "Essay on the Study of Literature:" "The primitive value of half a crown has risen to the fanciful price of a guinea or thirty shillings," or even more. I wish I had a copy myself, for old sake's sake.

Certain modern books, "on large paper," are safe investments. The "Badminton Library," an English series of books on sport, is at a huge premium already, when on "large paper." But one should never buy the book unless, as in the case of Dr. John Hill Burton's "Book-Hunter" (first edition), it is not only on large paper, and not only rare (twenty-five copies), but also readable and interesting. {7} A collector should have the taste to see when a new book is in itself valuable and charming, and when its author is likely to succeed, so that his early attempts (as in the case of Mr. Matthew Arnold, Lord Tennyson, and a few others of the moderns) are certain to become things of curious interest.

You can hardly ever get a novel of Jane Austen's in the first edition. She is rarer than Fielding or Smollett. Some day it may be the same in Miss Broughton's case. Cling to the fair and witty Jane, if you get a chance. Beware of illustrated modern books in which "processes" are employed. Amateurs will never really value mechanical reproductions, which can be copied to any extent. The old French copper-plate engravings and the best English mezzo-tints are so valuable because good impressions are necessarily so rare.

One more piece of advice. Never (or "hardly ever") buy an imperfect book. It is a constant source of regret, an eyesore. Here have I Lovelace's "Lucasta," 1649, *without the engraving*. It is deplorable, but I never had a chance of another "Lucasta." This is not a case of *invenies aliam*. However you fare, you will have the pleasure of Hope and the consolation of books *quietem inveniendam in abditis recessibus et libellulis*.

ROCHEFOUCAULD

To the Lady Violet Lebas.

Dear Lady Violet,—I am not sure that I agree with you in your admiration of Rochefoucauld—of the *Réflexions, ou Sentences et Maximes Morales,* I mean. At least, I hardly agree when I have read many of them at a stretch. It is not fair to read them in that way, of course, for there are more than five hundred *pensées,* and so much *esprit* becomes fatiguing. I doubt if people study them much. Five or six of them have become known even to writers in the newspapers, and we all copy them from each other.

Rochefoucauld says that a man may be too dull to be duped by a very clever person. He himself was so clever that he was often duped, first by the general honest dulness of mankind, and then by his own acuteness. He thought he saw more than he did see, and he said even more than he thought he saw. If the true motive of all our actions is self-love, or vanity, no man is a better proof of the truth than the great maxim-maker. His self-love took the shape of a brilliancy that is sometimes false. He is tricked out in paste for diamonds, now and then, like a vain, provincial beauty at a ball. "A clever man would frequently be much at a loss," he says, "in stupid company." One has seen this embarrassment of a wit in a company of dullards. It is Rochefoucauld's own position in this world of men and women. We are all, in the mass, dullards compared with his cleverness, and so he fails to understand us, is much at a loss among us. "People only praise others in hopes of being praised in turn," he says. Mankind is not such a company of "log-rollers" as he avers.

There is more truth in a line of Tennyson's about

> "The praise of those we love,
> Dearer to true young hearts than their own praise."

I venture to think we need not be young to prefer to hear the praise of others rather than our own. It is not embarrassing in the first place, as all praise of ourselves must be. I doubt if any man or woman can flatter so discreetly as not to make us uncomfortable. Besides, if our own performances be lauded, we are uneasy as to whether the honour is deserved. An artist has usually his own doubts about his own doings, or rather he has his own certainties. About our friends' work we need have no such misgivings. And our self-love is more delicately caressed by the success of our friends than by our own. It is still self-love, but it is filtered, so to speak, through our affection for another.

What are human motives, according to Rochefoucauld? Temperament, vanity, fear, indolence, self-love, and a grain of natural perversity, which somehow delights in evil for itself. He neglects that other element, a grain of natural worth, which somehow delights in good for itself. This taste, I think, is quite as innate, and as active in us, as that other taste for evil which causes there to be something not wholly displeasing in the misfortunes of our friends.

There is a story which always appears to me a touching proof of this grain of goodness, as involuntary, as fatal as its opposite. I do not remember in what book of travels I found this trait of native excellence. The black fellows of Australia are very fond of sugar, and no wonder, if it be true that it has on them an intoxicating effect. Well, a certain black fellow had a small parcel of brown sugar which was pilfered from his lair in the camp. He detected the thief, who was condemned to be punished according to tribal law; that is to say, the injured man was allowed to have a whack at his enemy's head with a waddy, a short club of heavy hard wood. The whack was duly given, and then the black who had suffered the loss threw down his club, burst into tears, embraced the thief and displayed every sign of a lively regret for his revenge.

That seems to me an example of the human touch that Rochefoucauld never allows for, the natural goodness, pity, kindness, which can assert itself in contempt of the love of self, and the love of revenge. This is that true clemency which is a real virtue, and not "the child of Vanity, Fear, Indolence, or of all three together." Nor is it so true that "we have all fortitude enough to endure the misfortunes of others." Everybody has witnessed another's grief that came as near him as his own.

How much more true, and how greatly poetical is that famous maxim: "Death and the Sun are two things not to be looked on with a steady eye." This version is from the earliest English translation of 1698. The *Maximes* were first published in Paris in 1665. {8} "Our tardy apish nation" took thirty-three years in finding them out and appropriating them. This, too, is good: "If we were faultless, we would observe with less pleasure the faults of others." Indeed, to observe these with pleasure is not the least of our faults. Again, "We are never so happy, nor so wretched, as we suppose." It is our vanity, perhaps, that makes us think ourselves *miserrimi*.

Do you remember—no, you don't—that meeting in "Candide" of the unfortunate Cunégonde and the still more unfortunate old lady who was the daughter of a Pope? "You lament your fate," said the old lady; "alas, you have known no such sorrows as mine!" "What! my good woman!" says Cunégonde. "Unless you have been maltreated by *two* Bulgarians, received *two* stabs from a knife, had *two* of your castles burned over your head, seen *two* fathers and *two* mothers murdered before your eyes, and *two* of your lovers flogged at two autos-da-fé, I don't fancy that you can have the advantage of me. Besides, I was born a baroness of seventy-two quarterings, and I have been a cook." But the daughter of a Pope had, indeed, been still more unlucky, as she proved, than Cunégonde; and the old lady was not a little proud of it.

But can you call *this* true: "There is nobody but is ashamed of having loved when once he loves no longer"? If it be true at all, I don't think the love was much worth having or giving. If one really loves once, one can never be ashamed of it; for we never cease to love. However, this is the very high water of sentiment, you will say; but I blush no more for it than M. le Duc de Rochefoucauld for his own opinion. Perhaps I am thinking of that kind of love about which he says: "True love is like ghosts; which everybody talks about and few have seen." "Many be the thyrsus-bearers, few the Mystics," as the Greek proverb runs. "Many are called, few are chosen."

As to friendship being "a reciprocity of interests," the saying is but one of those which Rochefoucauld's vanity imposed on his wit. Very witty it is not, and it is emphatically untrue. "Old men console themselves by giving good advice for being no longer able to set bad examples." Capital; but the poor old men are often good examples of the results of not taking their own good advice. "Many an ingrate is less to blame than his benefactor." One might add, at least I will, "Every man who looks for gratitude deserves to get none of it." "To say that one never flirts—is flirting." I rather like the old translator's version of "Il y a de bons mariages; mais il n'y en a point de délicieux"—"Marriage is sometimes convenient, but never delightful."

How true is this of authors with a brief popularity: "*Il y a des gens qui ressemblent aux vaudevilles, qu'on ne chante qu'un certain temps.*" Again, "to be in haste to repay a kindness is a sort of ingratitude," and a rather insulting sort too. "Almost everybody likes to repay small favours; many people can be grateful for favours not too weighty, but for favours truly great there is scarce anything but ingratitude." They must have been small favours that Wordsworth had conferred when "the gratitude of men had oftener left him mourning." Indeed, the very pettiness of the aid we can generally render each other, makes gratitude the touching thing it is. So much is repaid for so little, and few can ever have the chance of incurring the thanklessness that Rochefoucauld found all but universal.

"Lovers and ladies never bore each other, because they never speak of anything but themselves." Do husbands and wives often bore each other for the same reason? Who said: "To know all is to forgive all"? It is rather like "On pardonne tant que l'on aime"—"As long as we love we can forgive," a comfortable saying, and these are rare in Rochefoucauld. "Women do not quite know what flirts they are" is also, let us hope, not incorrect. The maxim that "There is a love so excessive that it kills jealousy" is only a corollary from "as long as we love, we forgive." You remember the classical example, Manon Lescaut and the Chevalier des Grieux; not an honourable precedent.

"The accent of our own country dwells in our hearts as well as on our tongues." Ah! never may I lose the Border accent! "Love's Miracle! To cure a coquette." "Most honest women are tired of their task," says this unbeliever. And the others? Are they never aweary? The Duke is his own best critic after all, when he says: "The greatest fault of a penetrating wit is going beyond the mark." Beyond the mark he frequently goes, but not when he says that we come as fresh hands to each new epoch of life, and often want experience for all our years. How hard it was to begin to be middle-aged! Shall we find old age easier if ever we come to its threshold? Perhaps, and Death perhaps the easiest of all. Nor let me forget, it will be long before *you* have occasion to remember, that "vivacity which grows with age is not far from folly."

OF VERS DE SOCIÉTÉ

To Mr. Gifted Hopkins.

My Dear Hopkins,—The verses which you have sent me, with a request "to get published in some magazine," I now return to you. If you are anxious that they should be published, send them to an editor yourself. If he likes them he will accept them from you. If he does not like them, why should he like them because they are forwarded by *me*? His only motive would be an aversion to disobliging a *confrère*, and why should I put him in such an unpleasant position?

But this is a very boorish way of thanking you for the *première représentation* of your little poem. "To Delia in Girton" you call it, "recommending her to avoid the Muses, and seek the society of the Graces and Loves." An old-fashioned preamble, and of the lengthiest, and how do you go on?—

> Golden hair is fairy gold,
>   Fairy gold that cannot stay,
> Turns to leaflets green and cold,
>   At the ending of the day!
>   Laurel-leaves the Muses may
> Twine about your golden head.
>   Will the crown reward you, say,
> When the fairy gold is fled?
>
> Daphne was a maid unwise—
>   Shun the laurel, seek the rose;
> Azure, lovely in the skies,
>   Shines less gracious in the hose!

Don't you think, dear Hopkins, that this allusion to *bas-bleus*, if not indelicate, is a little rococo, and out of date? Editors will think so, I fear. Besides, I don't like "Fairy gold *that cannot stay*." If *Fairy Gold* were a *horse*, it would be all very well to write that it "cannot stay." 'Tis the style of the stable, unsuited to songs of the *salon*.

This is a very difficult kind of verse that you are essaying, you whom the laurels of Mr. Locker do not suffer to sleep for envy. You kindly ask my opinion on *vers de société* in general. Well, I think them a very difficult sort of thing to write well, as one may infer from this, that the ancients, our masters, could hardly write them at all. In Greek poetry of the great ages I only remember one piece which can be called a model—the Æolic verses that Theocritus wrote to accompany the gift of the ivory distaff. It was a present, you remember, to the wife of his friend Nicias, the physician of Miletus. The Greeks of that age kept their women in almost Oriental reserve. One may doubt whether Nicias would have liked it if Theocritus had sent, instead of a distaff, a fan or a jewel. But there is safety in a spinning instrument, and all the compliments to the lady, "the dainty-ankled Theugenis," turn on her skill, and industry, and housewifery. So Louis XIV., no mean authority, called this piece of *vers de société* "a model of honourable gallantry."

I have just looked all through Pomtow's pretty little pocket volumes of the minor Greek poets, and found nothing more of the nature of the lighter verse than this of Alcman's—ου μ' ετι παρθενιϰαι. Do you remember the pretty paraphrase of it in "Love in Idleness"?

> "Maidens with voices like honey for sweetness that
> breathe desire,
> Would that I were a sea bird with wings that could never
> tire,
> Over the foam-flowers flying, with halcyons ever on wing,
> Keeping a careless heart, a sea-blue bird of the spring."

It does not quite give the sense Alcman intended, the lament for his limbs weary with old age—with old age sadder for the sight of the honey-voiced girls.

The Greeks had not the kind of society that is the home of "Society Verses," where, as Mr. Locker says, "a *boudoir* decorum is, or ought always to be, preserved, where sentiment never surges into passion, and where humour never overflows into boisterous merriment." Honest women were estranged from their mirth and their melancholy.

The Romans were little more fortunate. You cannot expect the genius of Catullus not to "surge into passion," even in his hours of gayer song, composed when

> *Multum lusimus in meis tabellis,*
> *Ut convenerat esse delicatos,*
> *Scribens versiculos uterque nostrum.*

Thus the lighter pieces of Catullus, like the dedication of his book, are addressed to *men*, his friends, and thus they scarcely come into the category of what we call "Society Verses." Given the character of Roman society, perhaps we might say that plenty of this kind of verse was written by Horace and by Martial. The famous ode to Pyrrha does not exceed the decorum of a Roman *boudoir*, and, as far as love was concerned, it does not seem to have been in the nature of Horace to "surge into passion." So his best songs in this kind are addressed to men, with whom he drinks a little, and talks of politics and literature a great deal, and muses over the shortness of life, and the zest that snow-clad Soracte gives to the wintry fire.

Perhaps the ode to Leuconoe, which Mr. Austin Dobson has rendered so prettily in a *villanelle*, may come within the scope of this Muse, for it has a playfulness mingled with its melancholy, a sadness in its play. Perhaps, too, if Horace is to be done into verse, these old French forms seem as fit vehicles as any for Latin poetry that was written in the exotic measures of Greece. There is a foreign grace and a little technical difficulty overcome in the *English ballade and villanelle*, as in the Horatian sapphics and alcaics. I would not say so much, on my own responsibility, nor trespass so far on the domain of scholarship, but this opinion was communicated to me by a learned professor of Latin. I think, too, that some of the lyric measures of the old French Pleiad, of Ronsard and Du Bellay, would be well wedded with the verse of Horace. But perhaps no translator will ever please any one but himself, and of Horace every man must be his own translator.

It may be that Ovid now and then comes near to writing *vers de société*, only he never troubles himself for a moment about the "decorum of the *boudoir*." Do you remember the lines on the ring which he gave his lady? They are the origin and pattern of all the verses written by lovers on that pretty metempsychosis which shall make them slippers, or fans, or girdles, like Waller's, and like that which bound "the dainty, dainty waist" of the Miller's Daughter.

> "Ring that shalt bind the finger fair
> Of my sweet maid, thou art not rare;
> Thou hast not any price above
> The token of her poet's love;
> Her finger may'st thou mate as she
> Is mated every wise with me!"

And the poet goes on, as poets will, to wish he were this favoured, this fortunate jewel:

> "In vain I wish! So, ring, depart,
> And say 'with me thou hast his heart'!"

Once more Ovid's verses on his catholic affection for all ladies, the brown and the blonde, the short and the tall, may have suggested Cowley's humorous confession, "The Chronicle":

> "Margarita first possessed,
> If I remember well, my breast,
> Margarita, first of all;"

and then follows a list as long as Leporello's.

What disqualifies Ovid as a writer of *vers de société* is not so much his lack of "decorum" as the monotonous singsong of his eternal elegiacs. The lightest of light things, the poet of society, should possess more varied strains; like Horace, Martial, Thackeray, not like Ovid and (here is a heresy) Praed. Inimitably well as Praed does his trick of antithesis, I still feel that it *is* a trick, and that most rhymers could follow him in a mere mechanic art. But here the judgment of Mr. Locker would be opposed to this modest opinion, and there would be opposition again where Mr. Locker calls Dr. O. W. Holmes "perhaps the best living writer of this species of verse." But here we are straying among the moderns before exhausting the ancients, of whom I fancy that Martial, at his best, approaches most near the ideal.

Of course it is true that many of Martial's lyrics would be thought disgusting in any well-regulated convict establishment. His gallantry is rarely "honourable." Scaliger used to burn a copy of Martial, once a year, on the altar of Catullus, who himself was far from prudish. But Martial, somehow, kept his heart undepraved, and his taste in books was excellent. How often he writes verses for the bibliophile, delighting in the details of purple and gold, the illustrations and ornaments for his new volume! These pieces are for the few—for amateurs, but we may all be touched by his grief for the little lass, Erotion. He commends her in Hades to his own father and mother gone before him, that the child may not be frightened in the dark, friendless among the shades

> "*Parvula ne nigras horrescat Erotion umbras*
> *Oraque Tartarei prodigiosa canis.*"

There is a kind of playfulness in the sorrow, and the pity of a man for a child; pity that shows itself in a smile. I try to render that other inscription for the tomb of little Erotion:

> Here lies the body of the little maid
>   Erotion;
> From her sixth winter's snows her eager shade
>   Hath fleeted on!
> Whoe'er thou be that after me shalt sway
>   My scanty farm,
> To her slight shade the yearly offering pay,
>   So—safe from harm—
> Shall thou and thine revere the kindly *Lar*,
>   And *this* alone
> Be, through thy brief dominion, near or far,
>   A mournful stone!

Certainly he had a heart, this foul-mouthed Martial, who claimed for the study of his book no serious hours, but moments of mirth, when men are glad with wine, "in the reign of the Rose:" {9}

> *"Hæc hora est tua, cum furit Lyæus,*
> *Cum regnat rosa, cum madent capilli;*
> *Tunc mevel rigidi legant Catones."*

But enough of the poets of old; another day we may turn to Carew and Suckling, Praed and Locker, poets of our own speech, lighter lyrists of our own time. {10}

ON VERS DE SOCIÉTÉ

To Mr. Gifted Hopkins.

Dear Gifted,—If you will permit me to use your Christian, and prophetic, name—we improved the occasion lately with the writers of light verse in ancient times. We decided that the ancients were not great in verses of society, because they had, properly speaking, no society to write verses for. Women did not live in the Christian freedom and social equality with men, either in Greece or Rome—at least not "modest women," as Mr. Harry Foker calls them in "Pendennis." About the others there is plenty of pretty verse in the Anthology. What you need for verses of society is a period in which the social equality is recognized, and in which people are peaceable enough and comfortable enough to "play with light loves in the portal" of the Temple of Hymen, without any very definite intentions, on either part, of going inside and getting married.

Perhaps we should not expect *vers de société* from the Crusaders, who were not peaceable, and who were very earnest indeed, in love or war. But as soon as you get a Court, and Court life, in France, even though the times were warlike, then ladies are lauded in artful strains, and the lyre is struck *leviore plectro*. Charles d'Orleans, that captive and captivating prince, wrote thousands of *rondeaux*; even before his time a gallant company of gentlemen composed the *Livre des Cent Ballades*, one hundred *ballades*, practically unreadable by modern men. Then came Clément Marot, with his gay and rather empty fluency, and Ronsard, with his mythological compliments, his sonnets, decked with roses, and led like lambs to the altar of Helen or Cassandra. A few, here and there, of his pieces are lighter, more pleasant, and, in a quiet way, immortal, such as the verses to his "fair flower of Anjou," a beauty of fifteen. So they ran on, in France, till Voiture's time, and Sarrazin's with his merry *ballade* of an elopement, and Corneille's proud and graceful stanzas to Marquise de Gorla.

But verses in the English tongue are more worthy of our attention. Mr. Locker begins his collection of them, *Lyra Elegantiarum* (no longer a very rare book in England), as far back as Skelton's age, and as Thomas Wyat's, and Sidney's; but those things, the lighter lyrics of that day, are rather songs than poems, and probably were all meant to be sung to the virginals by our musical ancestors.

"Drink to me only with thine eyes," says the great Ben Jonson, or sings it rather. The words, that he versified out of the Greek prose of Philostratus, cannot be thought of without the tune. It is the same with Carew's "He that loves a rosy cheek," or with "Roses, their sharp spines being gone." The lighter poetry of Carew's day is all powdered with gold dust, like the court ladies' hair, and is crowned and diapered with roses, and heavy with fabulous scents from the Arabian phoenix's nest. Little Cupids flutter and twitter here and there among the boughs, as in that feast of Adonis which Ptolemy's sister gave in Alexandria, or as in Eisen's vignettes for Dorat's *Baisers*:

> "Ask me no more whither do stray
> The golden atoms of the day;
> For in pure love did Heaven prepare
> These powders to enrich your hair."

It would be affectation, Gifted, if *you* rhymed in that fashion for the lady of your love, and presented her, as it were, with cosmical cosmetics, and compliments drawn from the starry spaces and deserts, from skies, phoenixes, and angels. But it was a natural and pretty way of writing when Thomas Carew was young. I prefer Herrick the inexhaustible in dainties; Herrick, that parson-pagan, with the soul of a Greek of the Anthology, and a cure of souls (Heaven help them!) in Devonshire. His Julia is the least mortal of these "daughters of dreams and of stories," whom poets celebrate; she has a certain opulence of flesh and blood, a cheek like a damask rose, and "rich eyes," like Keats's lady; no vaporous Beatrice, she; but a handsome English wench, with

> "A cuff neglectful and thereby
> Ribbons to flow confusedly;
> A winning wave, deserving note
> In the tempestuous petticoat."

Then Suckling strikes up a reckless military air; a warrior he is who has seen many a siege of hearts—hearts that capitulated, or held out like Troy-town, and the impatient assailant whistles:

> "Quit, quit, for shame: this will not move,
>   This cannot take her.
> If of herself she will not love,
>   Nothing can make her—
>   The devil take her."

So he rides away, curling his moustache, hiding his defeat in a big inimitable swagger. It is a pleasanter piece in which Suckling, after a long leaguer of a lady's heart, finds that Captain honour is governor of the place, and surrender hopeless. So he departs with a salute:

> "March, march (quoth I), the word straight give,
>   Let's lose no time but leave her:

That giant upon air will live,
    And hold it out for ever."

Lovelace is even a better type in his rare good things of the military amorist and poet. What apology of Lauzun's, or Bussy Rabutin's for faithlessness could equal this?—

"Why dost thou say I am forsworn,
    Since thine I vowed to be?
Lady, it is already morn;
    It was last night I swore to thee
    That fond impossibility."

Has "In Memoriam" nobler numbers than the poem, from exile, to Lucasta?—

"Our Faith and troth
All time and space controls,
Above the highest sphere we meet,
Unseen, unknown, and greet as angels greet."

How comes it that in the fierce fighting days the soldiers were so tuneful, and such scholars? In the first edition of Lovelace's "Lucasta" there is a flock of recommendatory verses, English, Latin, even Greek, by the gallant Colonel's mess-mates and comrades. What guardsman now writes like Lovelace, and how many of his friends could applaud him in Greek? You, my Gifted, are happily of a pacific disposition, and tune a gentle lyre. Is it not lucky for swains like you that the soldiers have quite forsworn sonneting? When a man was a rake, a poet, a warrior, all in one, what chance had a peaceful minor poet like you or me, Gifted, against his charms? Sedley, when sober, must have been an invincible rival— invincible, above all, when he pretended constancy:

"Why then should I seek further store,
    And still make love anew?
When change itself can give no more
    'Tis easy to be true."

How infinitely more delightful, musical, and captivating are those Cavalier singers—their numbers flowing fair, like their scented lovelocks—than the prudish society poets of Pope's day. "The Rape of the Lock" is very witty, but through it all don't you mark the sneer of the contemptuous, unmanly little wit, the crooked dandy? He jibes among his compliments; and I do not wonder that Mistress Arabella Fermor was not conciliated by his long-drawn cleverness and polished lines. I prefer Sackville's verses "written at sea the night before an engagement":

> "To all you ladies now on land
>   We men at sea indite."

They are all alike, the wits of Queen Anne; and even Matt Prior, when he writes of ladies occasionally, writes down to them, or at least glances up very saucily from his position on his knees. But Prior is the best of them, and the most candid:

> "I court others in verse—but I love thee in prose;
> And they have my whimsies, but thou hast my heart."

Yes, Prior is probably the greatest of all who dally with the light lyre which thrills to the wings of fleeting Loves—the greatest English writer of *vers de société*; the most gay, frank, good-humoured, tuneful and engaging.

Landor is great, too, but in another kind; the bees that hummed over Plato's cradle have left their honey on his lips; none but Landor, or a Greek, could have written this on Catullus:

> "Tell me not what too well I know
> About the Bard of Sirmio—
>   Yes, in Thalia's son
> Such stains there are as when a Grace
> Sprinkles another's laughing face
>   With nectar, and runs on!"

That is poetry deserving of a place among the rarest things in the Anthology. It is a sorrow to me that I cannot quite place Praed with Prior in my affections. With all his gaiety and wit, he wearies one at last with that clever, punning antithesis. I don't want to know how

> "Captain Hazard wins a bet,
>   Or Beaulieu spoils a curry"—

and I prefer his sombre "Red Fisherman," the idea of which is borrowed, wittingly or unwittingly, from Lucian.

Thackeray, too careless in his measures, yet comes nearer Prior in breadth of humour and in unaffected tenderness. Who can equal that song, "Once you come to Forty Year," or the lines on the Venice Love-lamp, or the "Cane-bottomed Chair"? Of living English writers of verse in the "familiar style," as Cowper has it, I prefer Mr. Locker when he is tender and not untouched with melancholy, as in "The Portrait of a Lady," and Mr. Austin Dobson, when he is not flirting, but in earnest, as in the "Song of Four Seasons" and "The Dead Letter." He has ingenuity, pathos, mastery of his art, and, though the least pedantic of poets, is "conveniently learned."

Of contemporary Americans, if I may be frank, I prefer the verse of Mr. Bret Harte, verse with so many tunes and turns, as comic as the "Heathen Chinee," as tender as the lay of the ship with its crew of children that slipped its moorings in the fog. To me it seems that Mr. Bret Harte's poems have never (at least in this country) been sufficiently esteemed. Mr. Lowell has written ("The Biglow Papers" apart) but little in this vein. Mr. Wendell Holmes, your delightful godfather, Gifted, has written much with perhaps some loss from the very quantity. A little of *vers de société*, my dear Gifted, goes a long way, as you will think, if ever you sit down steadily to read right through any collection of poems in this manner. So do not add too rapidly to your own store; let them be "few, but roses" all of them.

RICHARDSON

By Mrs. Andrew Lang.

Dear Miss Somerville,—I was much interested in your fruitless struggle to read "Sir Charles Grandison,"—the book whose separate numbers were awaited with such impatience by Richardson's endless lady friends and correspondents, and even by the rakish world—even by Colley Cibber himself. I sympathize entirely with your estimate of its dulness; yet, dull as it is, it is worth wading through to understand the kind of literature which could flutter the dove-cotes of the last century in a generation earlier than the one that was moved to tears by the wearisome dramas of Hannah More.

There is only one character in the whole of "Sir Charles Grandison" where Richardson is in the least like himself—in the least like the Richardson of "Pamela" and "Clarissa." This character is Miss Charlotte Grandison, the sister of Sir Charles, and later (after many vicissitudes) the wife of Lord G. Miss Grandison's conduct falls infinitely beneath the high standard attained to by the rest of Sir Charles's chosen friends. She is petulant and loves to tease; is uncertain of what she wants; she is lively and sarcastic, and, worse than all, abandons the rounded periods of her brother and Miss Byron for free, not to say slang, expressions. "Hang ceremony!" she often exclaims, with much reason, while "What a deuce!" is her favourite expletive.

The conscientious reader heaves a sigh of relief when this young lady and her many indiscretions appear on the scene; when Miss Grandison, like Nature, "takes the pen from Richardson and writes for him." But I gather that you, my dear Miss Somerville, never got far enough to make her acquaintance, and therefore are still ignorant of the singular qualities of her brother, Sir Charles—Richardson's idea of a perfect man, for both brother and sister are introduced at almost the same moment.

Now it is nearly as difficult to realize that Sir Charles is a young man of twenty-six, as it is to feel that his antithesis, the adorable Pepys of the "Diary," was of that precise age. Sir Charles might be borne with good-naturedly for a short time as an old gentleman who had become garrulous from want of contradiction, but in any other aspect he would be shunned conscientiously. Yet Richardson is not content with putting into his mouth lengthy discourses tending chiefly, though expressed with mock humility, to his own glorification; but he keeps all the other characters perpetually dancing round the Baronet in a chorus of praise. "Was there ever such a man, my Harriet, so good, so just, so noble in his sentiments?" "Ah, my

Lucy, dare I hope for the affection of the best of men?" Some people would have begged their friends to cease making them ridiculous, but not so Sir Charles.

But, my dear, trying as Sir Charles is at all moments, he is infinitely at his worst when he attempts to be jocose, when he rallies the step-mother of his friend Beauchamp in a sprightly manner, or exchanges quips with Harriet's cousins at the house of "that excellent ancient," her grandmother. It is a mammoth posing as a kitten, though whatever he says or does, his audience throw up their hands and eyes and ask: "Was there ever such a man?" "Thank Heaven, *never!*" the nineteenth century replies unanimously.

Secure as he is of the contemporary public verdict, Sir Charles does not attempt to repress his love of "pawing" all his female acquaintances. He is eternally taking their hands, putting his arm round their waists, leading them up and down, and permitting himself liberties that in a less perfect character would be considered intolerable. It is also interesting to note that he never addresses any of his female friends without the prefix "my." "My Harriet," "my Emily," "my Charlotte," are his usual forms, and he is likewise very much addicted to the use of the third person, which may, however, have been the result of his long residence in Italy.

Little as you read of the book, no doubt you were struck—you *must* have been—by the singular practice in this very matter of Christian names, and also by the enormous satisfaction with which every one promptly adopts every one else as his brother or sister. As regards names, no sooner has Sir Charles rescued Harriet from the clutches of Sir Hargrave Pollexfen, than he calls her "*his* Harriet," though, when he is once engaged to her, then this is changed into "infinitely obliging Miss Byron." His eldest sister, one year his senior, is always "Lady L." to him, and on her marriage "his Charlotte," aged twenty-four, becomes "Lady G.;" but no one ever ventures to address him with anything more familiar than "Sir Charles." Harriet, indeed, once gets as far as "my Cha-" but this was in a moment of extreme emotion— one of the excesses of youth.

Of course the method of telling his story in letters necessitates the acceptance of various improbabilities; reticence has sometimes to be violated, and confidences to be unduly made. Still, with all these allowances, the gossip of every one with regard to the likelihood of Sir Charles returning Harriet's very thinly veiled attachment is highly undignified, and often indecent. The Object himself, for whom no less than seven ladies were at that time openly sighing, alone ignores Harriet's love, or, at any rate, appears to do so. But his sisters freely and frequently charge her with having fallen in love with him. She writes pages to her whole family as to his behaviour on particular occasions, while his ward,

Emily Jervois, begs permission to take up her abode with Harriet when she and Sir Charles are married.

Miss Jervois, who is Richardson's idea of a *jeune personne bien élevée*, is a compound of tears, of servility, and of undisguised love for her guardian. She is much more like the heroine of a French drama than an English girl of fourteen, and I dread to think what effect she would have on a free-born American! Harriet, as you know, is not quite hopeless at first, but the descent is easy, and, in the end, we quite agree with all the admiring circle, that they were made for each other. They were equally pompous, and used stilts of equal height.

"Sir Charles Grandison" was the last, the most socially ambitious, and much the worst of Richardson's novel's. Smollett came to his best in his last, "Humphrey Clinker." Fielding sobered down into the kind excellence of *his* last, "Amelia." Neither had been flattered and coddled by literary ladies, like Richardson. What of "Pamela" and "Clarissa"? May a maiden read the book that the young lady studied over Charles Lamb's shoulder? Well, I think, as you have now passed your quarter of a century, it would do you no harm to read the other two, which are infinitely better than "Sir Charles." The worthy Miss Byron, aged only twenty, indeed, writes to her Lucy to remind her that "their grandmother had told them twenty and twenty frightful stories of the vile enterprises of men against innocent creatures," and that they can both "call to mind stories which had ended much worse than hers (the affair with Sir Hargrave Pollexfen) had done."

Grandmothers now choose other topics of conversation for their descendants, but in those old days when sedan-chairs made *enlèvements* so very easy, it was considered necessary to caution girls against all the possible wiles of man. Even little boys, strange as it may sound, were given "Pamela" to read after the Bible. More than this, one small creature, Harry Campbell by name, so young that he always spoke of himself as "little Harry," obtained the book by stealth in his guardian's house, and never stopped till he finished it. When Richardson, on being told of this, sent him a copy for his own, he nearly went out of his senses with delight.

Of course you know the outline of Pamela's story. How at eleven she was taken and educated by a lady, who on her death, when Pamela was sixteen, left her not only more beautiful, but more accomplished than any girl of her years. How Pamela's young master fell in love with her, persecuted her, and after moving adventures of all kinds, being convinced that she was not to be overcome, married her, and they lived happy, with one brief exception, ever after. The proper frame of mind in which to read "Pamela" is to consider it in the light of an historical joke.

The absolute want of dignity that is almost as marked a characteristic in Richardson as his lack of humour, shows itself again and again. After all, Mr. B. would never have married Pamela if he could have persuaded her to live with him in any other way; so the cringing gratitude expressed by Pamela and her parents to the "good gentleman" and the "dear obliger" is only revolting. No woman with any delicacy of feeling could have sat complacently at her own table, while her husband entertained his company with prolonged and minute accounts of his attempts on her virtue. Can you fancy Fielding composing such a scene, Fielding whom Richardson scouts as a profligate? It is impossible not to laugh at the bare idea; and no less funny are Pamela's poetical flights, especially when, like Hamilton of Bangour in exile, she paraphrases the paraphrase of the 137th Psalm, about her captivity in Lincolnshire. All through one has to remind one's self perpetually that Pamela must not be expected to behave like a lady, and that if her father had done as he ought and removed her from her place when she first told him of her uneasiness, there would have been no story at all, and some other book would have had to rank in the opinion of Richardson's adorers "next to the Bible."

Still, whatever may have to be said as to Richardson's subjects, he is never coarse in his treatment of them. The pursuit of Pamela by Mr. B., or of Clarissa by Lovelace, through eight volumes, may weary; it does not corrupt. No man or maid on earth could lay it to his charge that he or she had been corrupted by these books, while no man on earth could read "Clarissa" without being touched by the noble ending. If "Clarissa" had never been written we should have said that the good-natured, fussy, essentially middle-class bookseller, Samuel Richardson, was unable to draw a lady; and it is curious to see how Clarissa stands out, not only among Richardson's female characters, but among the female characters of all time; eminent she is for purity of soul, and nobility of feeling. There is no cant about her anywhere, no effort to pose or to strain after a state of mind which she cannot naturally experience. The business-like manner in which she makes her preparations for death have nothing sentimental about them, nothing that even faintly suggests the pretty death-beds with which Mr. Dickens and others have made us familiar; but I doubt if the most practical money-maker in Wall Street could read it without feeling uncomfortable.

How, after describing such a character as Clarissa, Richardson could turn to the whale-bone figures in "Sir Charles Grandison" is quite incomprehensible. Had he been ruined by his numerous female admirers and correspondents, or by his desire to become fashionable, or, as is most likely, by the wish to create in Sir Charles a virtuous foil to him whom he thought the wicked, witty, delightful, and detestable Lovelace? Whatever the reason, it is a thousand pities that he gave way to his impulse.

It would interest you as well as me to note little points of manners that are to be gathered from the three books. I have not time to write much more, but will tell you two or three that have struck me. If you read them, as I still hope you may, you will see what early risers they all are, even the wicked Mr. B.; while Clarissa, when in Dover Street, usually gives Lovelace his interviews at six in the morning. One hears of two-o'clock-in-the-morning courage. How much more wonderful is love that rises at six!

Richardson was a woman's novelist, as Fielding was a man's. I sometimes think of Dr. Johnson's *mot*: "Claret for boys, port for men, and," smiling, "brandy for heroes." So one might fancy him saying: "Richardson for women, Fielding for men, Smollett for ruffians," though some of *his* rough customers were heroes, too. But we now confine ourselves so closely to "the later writers" of Russia, France, England, America, that the woman who reads Richardson may be called heroic. "To the unknown heroine" I dedicate my respect, as the Athenians dedicated an altar to "the unknown hero." Will you be the heroine? I am afraid you won't!

GÉRARD DE NERVAL

To Miss Girton, Cambridge.

Dear Miss Girton,—Yes, I fancy Gérard de Nerval is one of that rather select party of French writers whom Mrs. Girton will allow you to read. But even if you read him, I do not think you will care very much for him. He is a man's author, not a woman's; and yet one can hardly say why. It is not that he offends "the delicacy of your sex," as Tom Jones calls it; I think it is that his sentiment, whereof he is full, is not of the kind you like. Let it be admitted that, when his characters make love, they might do it "in a more human sort of way."

In this respect, and in some others, Gérard de Nerval resembles Edgar Poe. Not that his heroes are always attached to a *belle morte* in some distant Aiden; not that they have been for long in the family sepulchre; not that their attire is a vastly becoming shroud—no, Aurélie and Sylvie, in *Les Filles de Feu*, are nice and natural girls; but their lover is not in love with them "in a human sort of way." He is in love with some vaporous ideal, of which they faintly remind him. He is, as it were, the eternal passer-by; he is a wanderer from his birth; he sees the old *château*, or the farmer's cottage, or even the bright theatre, or the desert tent; he sees the daughters of men that they are fair and dear, in moonlight, in sunlight, in the glare of the footlights, and he looks, and longs, and sighs, and wanders on his fatal path. Nothing can make him pause, and at last his urgent spirit leads him over the limit of this earth, and far from the human shores; his delirious fancy haunts graveyards, or the fabled harbours of happy stars, and he who rested never, rests in the grave, forgetting his dreams or finding them true.

All this is too vague for you, I do not doubt, but for me the man and his work have an attraction I cannot very well explain, like the personal influence of one who is your friend, though other people cannot see what you see in him.

Gérard de Nerval (that was only his pen-name) was a young man of the young romantic school of 1830; one of the set of Hugo and Gautier. Their gallant, school-boyish absurdities are too familiar to be dwelt upon. They were much of Scott's mind when he was young, and translated Bürger, and "wished to heaven he had a skull and cross-bones." Two or three of them died early, two or three subsided into ordinary literary gentlemen (like M. Maquet, lately deceased), two, nay three, became poets—Victor Hugo, Théophile Gautier, and Gérard de Nerval. It is not necessary to have heard of Gérard; even that queer sham, the lady of culture, admits without a blush that she knows not Gérard. Yet he is worth knowing.

What he will live by is his story of "Sylvie;" it is one of the little masterpieces of the world. It has a Greek perfection. One reads it, and however old one is, youth comes back, and April, and a thousand pleasant sounds of birds in hedges, of wind in the boughs, of brooks trotting merrily under the rustic bridges. And this fresh nature is peopled by girls eternally young, natural, gay, or pensive, standing with eager feet on the threshold of their life, innocent, expectant, with the old ballads of old France on their lips. For the story is full of those artless, lisping numbers of the popular French Muse, the ancient ballads that Gérard collected and put in the mouth of Sylvie, the pretty peasant girl.

Do you know what it is to walk alone all day on the Border, and what good company to you the burn is that runs beside the highway? Just so companionable is the music of the ballads in that enchanted country of Gérard's fancy, in the land of the Valois. All the while you read, you have a sense of the briefness of the pleasure, you know that the hero cannot rest here, that the girls and their loves, the cottage and its shelter, are not for him. He is only passing by, happy yet wistful, far untravelled horizons are alluring him, the great city is drawing him to herself and will slay him one day in her den, as Scylla slew her victims.

Conceive Gérard living a wild life with wilder young men and women in a great barrack of an old hotel that the painters amused themselves by decorating. Conceive him coming home from the play, or rather from watching the particular actress for whom he had a distant, fantastic passion. He leaves the theatre and takes up a newspaper, where he reads that tomorrow the Archers of Senlis are to meet the Archers of Loisy. These were places in his native district, where he had been a boy. They recalled many memories; he could not sleep that night; the old scenes flashed before his half-dreaming eyes. This was one of the visions.

"In front of a *château* of the time of Henri IV., a *château* with peaked lichen-covered roofs, with a facing of red brick varied by stonework of a paler hue, lay a wide, green lawn set round with limes and elms, and through the leaves fell the golden rays of the setting sun. Young girls were dancing in a circle on the mossy grass, to the sound of airs that their mothers had sung, airs with words so pure and natural that one felt one's self indeed in that old Valois land, where for a thousand years has beat the heart of France.

"I was the only boy in the circle whither I had led my little friend, Sylvie, a child of a neighbouring hamlet; Sylvie, so full of life, so fresh, with her dark eyes, her regular profile, her sunburnt face. I had loved nobody, I had seen nobody but her, till the daughter of the *château*, fair and tall, entered the circle of peasant girls. To obtain the right to join the ring she had to chant a scrap of a ballad. We sat round her, and in a fresh, clear voice she sang one of the old ballads of romance, full of love and sadness . . . As she sang, the shadow of the great trees grew deeper, and the broad light of the risen moon fell on her alone, she standing without the listening circle. Her song was over, and no one dared to break the silence. A light mist arose from the mossy ground, trailing over the grass. We seemed to be in Paradise."

So the boy twisted a wreath for this new enchantress, the daughter of a line of nobles with king's blood in her veins. And little brown, deserted Sylvie cried.

All this Gérard remembered, and remembering, hurried down to the old country place, and met Sylvie, now a woman grown, beautiful, unspoiled, still remembering the primitive songs and fairy tales. They walked together through the woods to the cottage of the aunt of Sylvie, an old peasant woman of the richer class. She prepared dinner for them, and sent De Nerval for the girl, who had gone to ransack the peasant treasures in the garret.

Two portraits were hanging there—one that of a young man of the good old times, smiling with red lips and brown eyes, a pastel in an oval frame. Another medallion held the portrait of his wife, gay, *piquante*, in a bodice with ribbons fluttering, and with a bird perched on her finger. It was the old aunt in her youth, and further search discovered her ancient festal-gown, of stiff brocade. Sylvie arrayed herself in this splendour; patches were found in a box of tarnished gold, a fan, a necklace of amber.

The holiday attire of the dead uncle, who had been a keeper in the royal woods, was not far to seek, and Gérard and Sylvie appeared before the aunt, as her old self, and her old lover. "My children!" she cried and wept, and smiled through her tears at the cruel and charming apparition of youth. Presently she dried her tears, and only remembered the pomp and pride of her wedding. "We joined hands, and sang the *naïve* epithalamium of old France, amorous, and full of flowery turns, as the Song of Songs; we were the bride and the bridegroom all one sweet morning of summer."

I translated these fragments long ago in one of the first things I ever tried to write. The passages are as touching and fresh, the originals I mean, as when first I read them, and one hears the voice of Sylvie singing:

> "*A Dammartin, l'y a trois belles filles,*
> *L'y en a z'une plus belle que le jour!*"

So Sylvie married a confectioner, and, like Marion in the "Ballad of Forty Years," "Adrienne's dead" in a convent. That is all the story, all the idyll. Gérard also wrote the idyll of his own delirium, and the proofs of it (*Le*

Rêve et la Vie) were in his pocket when they found him dead in La Rue de la Vieille Lanterne.

Some of his poems have a sweetness and careless grace, like the grace of his favourite old ballads. One cannot translate things like this:

> *"Où sont nos amoureuses?*
> *Elles sont au tombeau!*
> *Elles sont plus heureuses*
> *Dans un séjour plus beau."*

But I shall try the couplets on a Greek air:

> *"Neither good morn nor good night."*

> The sunset is not yet, the morn is gone;
> Yet in our eyes the light hath paled and passed;
> But twilight shall be lovely as the dawn,
> And night shall bring forgetfulness at last!

Gérard's poems are few; the best are his vision of a lady with gold hair and brown eyes, whom he had loved in an earlier existence, and his humorous little piece on a boy's love for a fair cousin, and on their winter walk together, and the welcome smell of roast turkey which greets them on the stairs, when they come home. There are also poems of his madness, called *Chimères*, and very beautiful in form. You read and admire, and don't understand a line, yet it seems that if we were a little more or a little less mad we would understand:

> *"Et j'ai deux fois vainqueur traversé l'Achéron:*
> *Modulant tour à tour sur la lyre d'Orphée*
> *Les soupirs de la sainte et les cris de la fée."*

Here is an attempt to translate the untranslatable, the sonnet called—

> *"El Desdichado."*

> I am that dark, that disinherited,
> That all dishonoured Prince of Aquitaine,
> The Star upon my scutcheon long hath fled;
> A black sun on my lute doth yet remain!
> Oh, thou that didst console me not in vain,
> Within the tomb, among the midnight dead,
> Show me Italian seas, and blossoms wed,
> The rose, the vine-leaf, and the golden grain.

Say, am I Love or Phoebus? have I been
Or Lusignan or Biron? By a Queen
   Caressed within the Mermaid's haunt I lay,
And twice I crossed the unpermitted stream,
And touched on Orpheus' lyre as in a dream,
   Sighs of a Saint, and laughter of a Fay!

ON BOOKS ABOUT RED MEN

To Richard Wilby, Esq., Eton College, Windsor.

My Dear Dick,—It is very good of you, among your severe studies at Eton, to write to your Uncle. I am extremely pleased to hear that your football is appreciated in the highest circles, and shall be happy to have as good an account of your skill in making Latin verses.

I am glad you like "She," Mr. Rider Haggard's book which I sent you. It is "something like," as you say, and I quite agree with you, both in being in love with the heroine, and in thinking that she preaches rather too much. But, then, as she was over two thousand years old, and had lived for most of that time among cannibals, who did not understand her, one may excuse her for "jawing," as you say, a good deal, when she met white men. You want to know if "She" is a true story. Of course it is!

But you have read "She," and you have read all Cooper's, and Marryat's, and Mr. Stevenson's books, and "Tom Sawyer," and "Huckleberry Finn," several times. So have I, and am quite ready to begin again. But, to my mind, books about "Red Indians" have always seemed much the most interesting. At your age, I remember, I bought a tomahawk, and, as we had also lots of spears and boomerangs from Australia, the poultry used to have rather a rough time of it.

I never could do very much with a boomerang; but I could throw a spear to a hair's breadth, as many a chicken had occasion to discover. When you go home for Christmas I hope you will remember that all this was very wrong, and that you will consider we are civilized people, not Mohicans, nor Pawnees. I also made a stone pipe, like Hiawatha's, but I never could drill a hole in the stem, so it did not "draw" like a civilized pipe.

By way of an awful warning to you on this score, and also, as you say you want a *true* book about Red Indians, let me recommend to you the best book about them *I* ever came across. It is called "A Narrative of the Captivity and Adventures of John Tanner, during Thirty Years' Residence among the Indians," and it was published at New York by Messrs. Carvill, in 1830.

If I were an American publisher, instead of a British author (how I wish I was!) I'd publish "John Tanner" again, or perhaps cut a good deal out, and make a boy's book of it. You are not likely to get it to buy, but Mr. Steevens, the American bookseller, has found me a copy. If I lend you it, will you be kind enough to illustrate it on separate sheets of paper, and not make drawings on the pages of the book? This will, in the long run, be more satisfactory to yourself, as you will be able to keep your pictures; for I want "John Tanner" back again: and don't lend him to your fag-master.

Tanner was born about 1780; he lived in Kentucky. Don't you wish you had lived in Kentucky in Colonel Boone's time? The Shawnees were roaming about the neighbourhood when Tanner was a little boy. His uncle scalped one of them. This made bad feeling between the Tanners and the Shawnees; but John, like any boy of spirit, wished never to learn lessons, and wanted to be an Indian brave. He soon had more of being a brave than he liked; but he never learned any more lessons, and could not even read or write.

One day John's father told him not to leave the house, because from the movements of the horses, he knew that Indians were in the woods. So John seized the first chance and nipped out, and ran to a walnut tree in one of the fields, where he began filling his straw hat with walnuts. At that very moment he was caught by two Indians, who spilled the nuts, put his hat on his head, and bolted with him. One of the old women of the tribe had lost her son, and wanted to adopt a boy, and so they adopted Johnny Tanner. They ran with him till he was out of breath, till they reached the Ohio, where they threw him into a canoe, paddled across, and set off running again.

In ten days' hard marching they reached the camp, and it was worse than going to a new school, for all the Indians kicked John Tanner about, and "their dance," he says, "was brisk and cheerful, *after the manner of the scalp dance!*" Cheerful for John! He had to lie between the fire and the door of the lodge, and every one who passed gave him a kick. One old man was particularly cruel. When Tanner was grown up, he came back to that neighbourhood, and the first thing he asked was, "Where is Manito-o-geezhik?"

"Dead, two months since."

"It is well that he is dead," said John Tanner. But an old female chief, Net-ko-kua, adopted him, and now it began to be fun. For he was sent to shoot game for the family. Could anything be more delightful? His first shot was at pigeons, with a pistol. The pistol knocked down Tanner; but it also knocked down the pigeon. He then caught martins—and measles, which was less entertaining. Even Indians have measles! But even hunting is not altogether fun, when you start with no breakfast and have no chance of supper unless you kill game.

The other Red Indian books, especially the cheap ones, don't tell you that very often the Indians are more than half-starved. Then some one builds a magic lodge, and prays to the Great Spirit. Tanner often did this, and he would then dream how the Great Spirit appeared to him as a beautiful young man, and told him where he would find game, and prophesied other events in his life. It is curious to see a white man taking to the Indian religion, and having exactly the same sort of visions as their red converts described to the Jesuit fathers nearly two hundred years before.

Tanner saw some Indian ghosts, too, when he grew up. On the bank of the Little Saskawjewun there was a capital camping-place where the Indians never camped. It was called *Jebingneezh-o-shin-naut*—"the place of two Dead Men." Two Indians of the same *totem* had killed each other there. Now, their *totem* was that which Tanner bore, the *totem* of his adopted Indian mother. The story was that if any man camped there, the ghosts would come out of their graves; and that was just what happened. Tanner made the experiment; he camped and fell asleep. "Very soon I saw the two dead men come and sit down by my fire opposite me. I got up and sat opposite them by the fire, and in this position I awoke." Perhaps he fell asleep again, for he now saw the two dead men, who sat opposite to him, and laughed and poked fun and sticks at him. He could neither speak nor run away. One of them showed him a horse on a hill, and said, "There, my brother, is a horse I give you to ride on your journey home, and on your way you can call and leave the horse, and spend another night with us." So, next morning, he found the horse and rode it, but he did not spend another night with the ghosts of his own *totem*. He had seen enough of them.

Though Tanner believed in his own dreams of the Great Spirit, he did *not* believe in those of his Indian mother. He thought she used to prowl about in the daytime, find tracks of a bear or deer, watch where they went to, and then say the beast's lair had been revealed to her in a dream. But Tanner's own visions were "honest Injun." Once, in a hard winter, Tanner played a trick on the old woman. All the food they had was a quart of frozen bears' grease, kept in a kettle with a skin fastened over it. But Tanner caught a rabbit alive and popped him under the skin. So when the old woman went for the bears' grease in the morning, and found it alive, she was not a little alarmed.

But does not the notion of living on frozen pomatum rather take the gilt off the delight of being an Indian? The old woman was as brave and resolute as a man, but in one day she sold a hundred and twenty beaver skins and many buffalo robes for rum. She always entertained all the neighbouring Indians as long as the rum lasted, and Tanner had a narrow escape of growing up a drunkard. He became such a savage that when an Indian girl carelessly allowed his wigwam to be burned, he stripped her of her blanket and turned her out for the night in the snow.

So Tanner grew up in spite of hunger and drink. Once, when starving, and without bullets, he met a buck moose. If he killed the moose he would be saved, if he did not he would die. So he took the screws out of the lock of his rifle, loaded with them in place of bullets, tied the lock on with string, fired, and killed the moose.

Tanner was worried into marrying a young squaw (at least *he* says he did it because the girl wanted it), and this led to all his sorrows—this and a quarrel with a medicine-man. The medicine-man accused him of being a wizard, and his wife got another Indian to shoot him. Tanner was far from surgeons, and he actually hacked out the bullet himself with an old razor. Another wounded Indian once amputated his own arm. The ancient Spartans could not have been pluckier. The Indians had other virtues as well as pluck. They were honest and so hospitable, before they knew white men's ways, that they would give poor strangers new mocassins and new buffalo cloaks.

Will it bore you, my dear Dick, if I tell you of an old Indian's death? It seems a pretty and touching story. Old Pe-shau-ba was a friend of Tanner. One day he fell violently ill. He sent for Tanner and said to him: "I remember before I came to live in this world, I was with the Great Spirit above. I saw many good and desirable things, and among others a beautiful woman. And the Great Spirit said: 'Pe-shau-ba, do you love the woman?' I told him I did. Then he said, 'Go down and spend a few winters on earth. You cannot stay long, and you must remember to be always kind and good to my children whom you see below.' So I came down, but I have never forgotten what was said to me.

"I have always stood in the smoke between the two bands when my people fought with their enemies . . . I now hear the same voice that talked to me before I came into the world. It tells me I can remain here no longer." He then walked out, looked at the sun, the sky, the lake, and the distant hills; then came in, lay down composedly in his place, and in a few minutes ceased to breathe.

If we would hardly care to live like Indians, after all (and Tanner tired of it and came back, an old man, to the States), we might desire to die like Pe-shau-ba, if, like him, we had been "good and kind to God's children whom we meet below." So here is a Christmas moral for you, out of a Red Indian book, and I wish you a merry Christmas and a happy New Year.

APPENDIX I

Reynolds's Peter Bell.

When the article on John Hamilton Reynolds ("A Friend of Keats") was written, I had not seen his "Peter Bell" (Taylor and Hessey, London, 1888). This "Lyrical Ballad" is described in a letter of Keats's published by Mr. Sidney Colvin in *Macmillan's Magazine*, August, 1888. The point of Reynolds's joke was to produce a parody before the original. Reynolds was annoyed by what Hood called "The Betty Foybles" of Wordsworth, and by the demeanour of a poet who was serious, not only in season, but out of season. Moreover, Wordsworth had damned "a pretty piece of heathenism" by Keats, with praise which was faint even from Wordsworth to a contemporary. In the circumstances, as Wordsworth was not yet a kind of solemn shade, whom we see haunting the hills, and hear chanting the swan song of the dying England, perhaps Reynolds's parody scarce needs excuse. Mr. Ainger calls it "insolent," meaning that it has an unkind tone of personal attack. That is, unluckily, true, but to myself the parody appears remarkably funny, and quite worthy of "the sneering brothers, the vile Smiths," as Lamb calls the authors of "Rejected Addresses." Lamb wrote to tell Wordsworth that he did not see the fun of the parody— perhaps it is as well that we should fail to see the fun of jests broken on our friends. But will any Wordsworthian deny to-day the humour of this?—

> "He is rurally related;
> Peter Bell hath country cousins,
> (He had once a worthy mother),
> Bells and Peters by the dozens,
> But Peter Bell he hath no brothers,
> Not a brother owneth he,
> Peter Bell he hath no brother;
> His mother had no other son,
> No other son e'er called her 'mother,'
> Peter Bell hath brother none."

As Keats says in a review he wrote for *The Examiner*, "there is a pestilent humour in the rhymes, and an inveterate cadence in some of the stanzas that must be lamented." In his review Keats tried to hurt neither side, but his heart was with Reynolds; "it would be just as well to trounce Lord Byron in the same manner."

People still make an outcry over the trouncing of Keats. It was bludgeonly done, but only part of a game, a kind of horseplay at which most men of letters of the age were playing. Who but regrets that, in his "Life of Keats," Mr. Colvin should speak as if Sir Walter Scott had, perhaps, a guilty knowledge of the review of Keats in *Blackwood*! There is but a tittle of published evidence to the truth of a theory in itself utterly detestable, and, to every one who understands the character of Scott, wholly beyond possibility of belief. Even if Lockhart was the reviewer, and if Scott came to know it, was Scott responsible for what Lockhart did in 1819 or 1820, the very time when Mrs. Shelley thought he was defending Shelley in *Blackwood* (where he had praised her *Frankenstein*), and when she spoke of Sir Walter as "the only liberal man in the faction"? Unluckily Keats died, and his death was absurdly attributed to a pair of reviews which may have irritated him, and which were coarse, and cruel even for that period of robust reviewing. But Keats knew very well the value of these critiques, and probably resented them not much more than a football player resents being "hacked" in the course of the game. He was very willing to see Byron and Wordsworth "trounced," and as ready as Peter Corcoran in his friend's poem to "take punishment" himself. The character of Keats was plucky, and his estimate of his own genius was perfectly sane. He knew that he was in the thick of a literary "scrimmage," and he was not the man to flinch or to repine at the consequences.

APPENDIX II

Portraits of Virgil and Lucretius.

In the Letter on Virgil some remarks are made on a bust of the poet. It is wholly fanciful. Our only vestiges of a portrait of Virgil are in two MSS.; the better of the two is in the Vatican. The design represents a youth, with dark hair and a pleasant face, seated reading. A desk is beside him, and a case for manuscript, in shape like a band-box. (See Visconti, "Icon. Rom." i. 179, plate 13.) Martial tells us that portraits of Virgil were illuminated on copies of his "Æneid." The Vatican MS. is of the twelfth century. But every one who has followed the fortunes of books knows that a kind of tradition often preserves the illustrations, which are copied and recopied without material change. (See Mr. Jacobs's "Fables of Bidpai," Nutt, 1888.) Thus the Vatican MS. may preserve at least a shadow of Virgil.

If there be any portrait of Lucretius, it is a profile on a sard, published by Mr. Munro in his famous edition of the poet. The letters LVCR are inscribed on the stone, and appear to be contemporary with the gem. This, at least, is the opinion of Mr. A. S. Murray, of the late Mr. C. W. King, Braun, and Müller. On the other hand, Bernouilli ("Rom. Icon." i. 247) regards this, and apparently most other Roman gems with inscriptions, as "apocryphal." The ring, which was in the Nott collection, is now in my possession. If Lucretius were the rather pedantic and sharp-nosed Roman of the gem, his wife had little reason for the jealousy which took so deplorable a form. Cold this Lucretius may have been, volatile—never! {11}

FOOTNOTES

{1} This was written during the lifetime of Mr. Arnold and Mr. Browning.

{2} Since this was written, Mr. Bridges has made his lyrics accessible in "Shorter Poems." (G. Bell and Sons: 1890)

{3} Macmillans.

{4} Reynolds was, perhaps, a little irreverent. He anticipated Wordsworth's "Peter Bell" by a premature parody, "Peter Bell the First."

{5} Appendix on Reynolds's "Peter Bell."

{6} "Aucassin and Nicolette" has now been edited, annotated, and equipped with a translation by Mr. F. W. Bourdillon (Kegan Paul & Trench, 1887).

{7} Edinburgh, 1862.

{8} The Elzevir piracy was rather earlier.

{9} Pindar, perhaps, in one of his fragments, suggested that pretty *Cum regnat Rosa.*

{10} See next letter.

{11} Mr. Munro calls the stone "a black agate," and does not mention its *provenance.* The engraving in his book does no justice to the portrait. There is another gem representing Lucretius in the Vatican: of old it belonged to Leo X. The two gems are in all respects similar. A seal with this head, or one very like it, belonged to Evelyn, the friend of Mr. Pepys.

Lightning Source UK Ltd.
Milton Keynes UK
UKHW010647291222
414571UK00004B/175

9 789356 783164